BETTER THAN WORKING

THE MACMILLAN COMPANY
NEW YORK · CHICAGO
DALLAS · ATLANTA · SAN FRANCISCO
LONDON · MANILA

IN CANADA
BRETT-MACMILLAN LTD.
GALT, ONTARIO

PATRICK SKENE CATLING

BETTER THAN WORKING

New York   The Macmillan Company   1960

© Patrick Skene Catling 1960

First Printing

The Macmillan Company, New York
Brett-Macmillan Ltd., Galt, Ontario

Printed in the United States of America

Library of Congress catalog card number: 60-12171

dedicated with respect and affection to
FRANK R. KENT
JOHN W. OWENS
MARK S. WATSON
        and with special thanks to
CHARLES H. DORSEY, JR.

BETTER THAN WORKING

1

My earliest memory, a mere lantern slide of the mind compared with the Cinerama images of later years, is of me in a barrow being wheeled through an apple orchard in Normandy. I have enjoyed travel ever since, especially when indolently recumbent. As James M. Cannon III, of *Newsweek*, has said time and time again, "If you can't go first class, don't go"—words to live by, at least in principle. In practice I have not always been free to choose whether to go or stay. During my English school days there were family journeys to the Continent. During the Second World War, as a navigator, I was required to ferry aircraft from the Bahamas to Africa and India and from Canada to Scotland. I suffered a surfeit of mathematics and learned to distrust machines, but I increased my passion for maps and for acquiring a private empire by marking my routes on them.

After the war I returned with insufficient academic fervor to Oberlin College, in Ohio, and studied Modern English Poetry, Roman Daily Life, Astronomy, Charcoal Drawing, and beer. Mastery of these subjects may not seem to constitute an ideal preparation for a career in journalism. But what else are they a preparation for? The combination of an education that may be described most charitably as motley and a temperament that has moved me usually to feel nostalgia for the place just left behind, optimism for the place ahead, and a restless discontent with the immediate environment virtually forced me to become a newspaper reporter. In no other occupation is the present more fleeting.

My father was a reporter who wrote well. At home at times of professional frustration, he occasionally irritably warned me against getting mixed up with any part of the business; but the warnings seemed to lack sincerity. Somehow, I don't know how, it was understood that I would eventually drift into newspapers. At times, my father's encouragement, without ever reaching great heights of lyricism, was expressed in terms I found irresistible: "At least you'll get free tickets for first nights, and pencils and paper and typewriter ribbons and carbon paper." Stationery supplies in bulk have always exerted a powerful attraction on me. "Of course," he added, "if you want to be rich. . . ." He managed to suggest that making enough money with which to *buy* whatever one wanted was at best rather caddish, if not actually downright immoral. If I wasn't going to be a reporter, the only alternative, apparently, was to be a stockbroker with a black silk hat and a big cigar, as caricatured by David Low in some of his more bitter drawings during the Depression. This alternative was secretly tempting; but I faced the fact that I didn't know even how to begin to grind the faces of the poor.

My father died in Arizona. He had left his last newspaper job because of an illness, incorrectly diagnosed, as it turned out, that the hot, dry climate of Arizona was supposed to cure. His small capital, in pounds, was released slowly by the Bank of England, and spent rapidly in dollars. He had a grapefruit tree and an orange tree in the garden; but he became anxious about my mother and two younger brothers, and, in order to supplement his dwindling resources, submitted to the indignity of working as an "editorial adviser" to an eccentric old woman who published a pretentious little magazine.

Even so, he never tried to persuade me to get into steel or agriculture or advertising. To the contrary, the last professional advice he gave me before he died was more fervent than his rare advice of this kind had been in the past.

"There are two important things you must remember," he said. "For heaven's sake, never write for a news agency; and always spend as much time as you possibly can away from the home office. I think you'll like it. It's better than working."

2

I took a Baltimore & Ohio Railroad train from New York to Baltimore in September, 1947, at the age of twenty-two, for an interview with Charles H. Dorsey, Jr., who had recently been appointed managing editor of *The Sun*. The interview had been arranged by means of a brief, noncommittal exchange of letters. There was no way of knowing what to expect and I was nervous.

Walking down Charles Street toward the old Sunpapers' office, I felt a spasm of self-conscious horror. I had brought with me a scrapbook, bound in imitation red leather, containing clippings of everything I had ever written or drawn for publication: a parody of "Hiawatha" and an essay on "Homecoming" for *The Gower*, the magazine of University College School, London; a grotesque ink drawing for *The* (English) *Mickey Mouse Weekly*; cartoons and articles for the Bronxville (N.Y.) High School *Mirror* and school news for the Bronxville *Reporter*; letters to the editor and a "guest column" for the Oberlin *Review*; and news and feature articles, with emphasis on the activities of local advertisers, for the Pelham (N.Y.) *Sun*. At the

4

time of publication each piece had been read and reread with pride; now, as I carried the pathetic, intimate scraps up to Mr. Dorsey's office, I was sweating with shame. Perhaps I could leave the book with the elevator operator? I could not; they were my only credentials, the only evidence I could offer to support my claim, which suddenly seemed so specious, that I was an apprentice reporter. What if Mr. Dorsey should turn first to the picture from *The Mickey Mouse Weekly?*

Mr. Dorsey was not in his office when I arrived, one minute before the time of our appointment.

"He suggested that you go and have some lunch and come back in about an hour," his secretary said. I tried not to show how appalled I was by the thought of enduring further suspense.

"Could you recommend a nearby restaurant?" I asked lightly. "A reasonable one."

"The Lord Baltimore's just across the street," she said. "Your lunch will go on your expense account," she added with an encouraging smile.

With a dry mouth I chewed what might as well have been a heap of hardtack, and rehearsed silently the clever remarks that might help to save me from total humiliation. I tried to convince myself that I didn't need the job. After all, at that time there was a boom in housing construction; I could carry bricks.

By the time the interview took place, not in Mr. Dorsey's private office, but exposed at a desk in the news room, I was in such a state of mental paralysis that I could say hardly anything. Mr. Dorsey himself is not noted for garrulousness. We sat opposite each other murmuring occasional monosyllables; now and then he uttered a muffled snort.

"Well," he said at length, "just what makes you want a job in *Baltimore?*"

As at that time I knew nothing worth mentioning about H. L. Mencken, the Naval Academy, soft-shelled crabs, the Johns Hopkins University, the Maryland Club and Pimlico, or even the Baltimore *Sun,* except vaguely that it was supposed to be a good paper, I was at a loss for a reply.

"New York's so big. . . ."

5

"Humph," Dorsey snorted. "Things move pretty fast around here sometimes."

"Oh, yes," I agreed desperately; "I didn't mean that at all belittlingly." Now I sounded pompous, condescending. "I mean, I really like provinc—, that is, cities that are a bit less hectic than New York."

"Hmmm." He looked up at the clock and frowned.

"Have you done any writing?" he asked. I hesitantly lifted the scrapbook from my lap, opened it as though by chance at the carefully marked page of a signed article on a Westchester phonograph-record factory, and handed the book over. He riffled through it in the brisk manner of a customs inspector who obviously doesn't suspect that you have anything that you should have declared.

"Mm," he said, handing it back. "Yes. Thank you."

"Don't you want to read any of it?" I asked, temporarily forgetting that, a few moments before, the last thing in the world I had wanted was a reading. "I could leave it with you, if you like."

"No, that's all right," he assured me emphatically. "Look, er, Mr. . . . —as I told you in my letter, as you may recall, there is no immediate opening on the paper. But if one should come up, I'll let you know. Tell Mrs. Johnston how much today has cost you. She'll take you to the cashier." He stood up and I stood up and we shook hands and I thanked him and walked away. It was over.

When the secretary, the elevator man and the cashier smiled, it seemed to me that the interview must be already the talk, the joke, of the whole building.

I couldn't have been more surprised than I was when I got back to our apartment in Bronxville and my mother said there was a telegram for me.

"Can offer you forty-five a week to start," it said. "If interested wire when you can come. Other details can be talked about later. Anxious to have you. Regards—Dorsey."

That telegram after that interview still baffles me. But when I received the invitation I did not hesitate for a minute. After I had telegraphed my acceptance I did some joyful arithmetic. During the few weeks I had spent writing for the Pelham *Sun* I had been paid $25 a week. Now the Baltimore *Sun* was going to pay me $45! That would be over $180 a month—$2,340 a year!

6

But what were the other details? So far there had been no mention of any details. What would they expect me to do for that kind of money?

I went back to Baltimore a week later, and gradually I found out.

3

The main room of the police station at Pennsylvania Avenue and Dolphin Street, in a Negro section of northwestern Baltimore, was like an underendowed charitable institution.

White fluorescent lights emphasized its bareness and the darkness of the paint. The excessive steam heat, rumbling and rattling through the pipes and hissing from the safety valves of the radiators, intensified the thick, sweet smell of floor wax, the chemical smell of antiseptic, the faint, musty smell of decay, and the whiffs of ammoniacal pungency that seeped in when the door to the cell block was opened. It was a poor room with a high gloss. While the turnkey, an inferior policeman with an indoor complexion and a dark gray cardigan, mopped and polished the linoleum, one imagined rats and termites gnawing below.

This room was animated with the harsh jollity of a barrack three times a day when shifts were changing and patrolmen assembled to receive their orders, and some, laboriously, with much slow licking of lips, wrote out their reports.

Now, a wet evening in autumn, the room was almost empty and almost silent. It was separated into two parts by a high counter across one end. A sergeant in uniform was writing in the docket. Behind him, in a corner, a radio operator in shirt sleeves sat reading a book while his radios hummed and crackled as though at rest but irritable. Against the wall at the opposite end of the room there was a small table bearing a telephone that belonged to the Baltimore *Sun*. I was sitting at this table drawing triangles and cylinders and cones on folded copy paper and waiting for something to happen.

"Here's a good one," said the radio operator, turning from his radios with a book in his hand.

"Huh?" said the sergeant. He swiveled heavily around in his chair, peered over his steel spectacles at the book, and read aloud: " 'Homicidal Investigation: autopsies; what can be deduced from gunshot wounds. . . .' "

"Ain't that a dilly though?" the radio operator asked. He showed the sergeant a color photograph of what had been a man's face. Half the portrait was cerebral hemorrhage; the rest was animal alarm.

"This illustrates when fired at close range the effects of a shotgun may be devastating," the radio operator said with a proprietary smile. "Look—there's a worse one than that." His eyes were shining as he licked a plump finger and flicked over the pages to a picture of a man who had suffered "direct violence." The sergeant leaned closer.

" 'Strange to say,' " he read, " 'the victim was alive and perfectly conscious for several hours after receiving this injury.' Well, how about that? Wonder what he thought must of happened to him." The sergeant sounded faintly awed. He looked up and saw the radio operator's expression of satisfaction. "What are you trying to do?" the sergeant asked, belligerently jocular, "learn how to be a detective?"

The city editor had said that police reporting was the foundation on which all journalism was based. "Succeed as a police reporter," he had said, "and you'll be able to do anything. The first thing a police reporter must do is to get to know the cops. Humor them. Listen to all they have to say. They can help you a lot—or make things very difficult. . . ."

9

When the sergeant had returned with a grunt of martyrdom to his clerical duties, I went over to the counter and asked the radio operator as respectfully as possible whether I could look at his book.

"Yeah," he said, smiling again, beaming. "Sure. I got just the picture for you. A beaut." He found the page he was looking for. "Seventy-eight," he said. "Take a gander at seventy-eight." He closed the book and skimmed it so that it landed on the counter with a loud slap. The sergeant looked up sharply at me, then over his shoulder at the radio operator, but said nothing.

I turned the glossy pages, past unimaginable mutilations, to the recommended picture. Page seventy-eight illustrated the possibility of fatal stabbing with an ordinary safety pin. The page was filled with a photograph of a woman's breast. It was a good enough breast. In any other book it might have seemed a quite pleasant breast. But in that book it seemed monstrous.

"Aw, shucks," said the radio operator with mock tenderness, "I see I shocked you. You a bottle baby?" He bared his blue-white false teeth, as regular as a row of Chiclets. The joke had gone over just the way he liked it. Perhaps by Dale Carnegie standards I was accumulating credit.

There were noises of scuffling on the station steps. Two patrolmen appeared, breathing hard, dragging a reluctant Negro by the arms. He was leaning back, his head forward, and he was kicking at the shiny floor, but his shoes were slipping on it. I noticed the turnkey's look of fury as long, dull streaks were scraped on the linoleum.

The Negro failed to check his progress to the desk. He was elderly —his close-cropped hair looked like steel wool—but he seemed very strong. His shabby coat was taut against his back, and a vein in one temple was distended with the effort of resistance. One of the patrolmen was holding the prisoner by something resembling a single handcuff with a handle. There were new smells in the room: sweat and wine.

The Negro's eyes were closed. When he raised his head and blinked in the direction of the nearest fluorescent tubes it was possible to see that his eyes were rheumy white blanks. It was strange to see a blind man under arrest. I had always assumed that blind men were helpless, virtuous, patient philosophers, even on rainy nights when nobody bought their matches.

At last the police had him pressed securely against the brass rail that extended from the top of the counter, and the Negro, holding on to it, suddenly seemed acquiescent.

"Jeez," said one of the patrolmen, speaking over the bowed head. "I thought we'd never get him here. Mean sonevabitch, huh?" The other patrolman was holding the handcuff with one hand and wiping the back of his neck with a handkerchief. His face was red and moist. He put the handkerchief in his pocket. He raised his cap by its shiny black peak and with a couple of free fingers scratched his scalp. "Didn't like to hit him," he said. "Real stupid, he is. What you going to do?"

The sergeant carefully blotted what he had written in the docket and looked mildly over his glasses.

"Well," he said, "what's he here for?"

"Disorderly conduct, sergeant. Creating a disturbance outside a shoeshine parlor in the eighteen hundred block Pennsylvania. He's loaded."

There was a sudden ripple of energy through the Negro's body; it was with difficulty that the patrolmen restrained him. Something that one of them did made him wince and shudder and clench his teeth and then he was still and meek.

"All right," the sergeant said severely; "name?" There was no reply. The Negro's forehead was resting on the brass rail, a sweaty forehead on the turnkey's polished brass.

"Hey, you!" one of the patrolmen yelled into the prisoner's ear. "What's your name?"

"O.K., let him sleep it off," said the sergeant.

"Look him over good, Ed," he told the turnkey. "I don't want him cutting his throat."

The turnkey frisked the prisoner with malevolent vigor. The search produced a pink celluloid comb with two broken teeth, a small harmonica and about $1.50 in silver.

When the patrolmen returned from the cells, one of them was

adjusting his necktie and the other was fastidiously picking small pieces of skin from the inside of the handcuff. He saw that I was watching.

"I'm going to have to wash this goddamn thing," he said. "I wonder how many times I've told them: 'If you don't struggle you won't get hurt.'" He raised his eyebrows at a sudden inhuman bellow from a concrete echo chamber behind closed doors. "Ed's really pissed off about something tonight," he commented, then returned his attention to the handcuff.

"Look," he said to me, as kindly as a father explains a toy to a child. "See what happens when you pull against this thing?" He squeezed the steel ring and there were sharp clicks as teeth sprang locking the handcuff at a reduced diameter. "The more you pull, the tighter it gets. You understand?"

A short time later there was another demonstration. The man under arrest was white. There was no discrimination to speak of.

It was quiet in the police station, except for the creaking tread of policemen off duty walking around the pool table upstairs. My telephone rang. It was the city desk. A rewrite man said without reproach that I hadn't called for several hours. Did I have anything for him? I told him about the men that had been brought in and about the terrible cry I had heard. Could that sort of thing be reported?

"We don't bother about drunks," the rewrite man said, "except now and then when there are some good quotes in a magistrate's court."

"By the way," he said, "I wonder if you'd go down to South Baltimore General? Russ is having dinner. A private plane crashed and the casualties should be arriving just about now. We want the names and where they're from."

At the hospital it was difficult to get information. I badgered a nurse in the accident ward until she was rude. Then, walking along a corridor toward the ambulance entrance, I happened to see the room that the casualties had been wheeled into.

On a white table lay two men. There was something wrong with their necks, and their feet hung heavily over the end of the table like the leaden feet of marionettes.

"Are they badly injured?" I asked a man in a white coat who was leaning over the table. The doctor gave a short, humorless laugh. "They're dead," he said.

They were the first bodies I'd ever seen. We hadn't gone in for that sort of thing much in my part of the Air Force. My inexperience must have been apparent: the doctor became helpful, giving me the names and even supplying facts that I failed to ask for.

"There's a public telephone in the reception room," he said.

But the city desk was not interested.

"Just give us enough for a four-head," an assistant city editor said. "We've got a good murder in the Eastern District." The rewrite man came in on the line.

"Russ is back," he said. "You can go eat now."

4

My aptitude for police reporting was limited, no doubt, by a number of factors; however, I like to think that not the least of these was a rapidly diminishing sympathy with the police. I came to welcome the ringing of the police stations' automatic electric bells signaling fire alarms. There was a refreshing moral clarity about fire-fighting, an elemental conflict between water and fire, between good and evil; and, though the conflict was occasionally a fierce one, the victory was as sure as the virtuous cowboys' triumph in a classic Western. Compared with sitting in a police station, it seemed not at all unpleasant to stand in a suburban street at night, sipping coffee that tasted like hot cardboard, watching a Niagara of diamonds fall through the searchlights' beams while men in black oilskins and smoke masks axed holes in the roof of a Baltimore colonial mansionette whose inhabitants had reported a flickering pilot light in the kitchen stove. It was especially gratifying to watch the forces of righteousness blasting away when one learned that the building being saved was fully insured.

The most loathesome assignments ever inflicted on police reporters are intrusions into the homes of the next of kin of criminals or the victims of criminals. Generally speaking, *The Sun* is less offensive than most other papers in this way; but overzealous junior editors, sitting beyond embarrassment in the security of the news room, occasionally violate the temperate spirit of the paper by ordering a reporter to interview the mother of a youth condemned to death, say, or the mother of a girl who has been raped and murdered. (Mothers are always preferred for this ghoulish sort of enterprise; they weep more gently than fathers and talk more.)

After having applied to a bereaved family for a portrait of a murdered child, which, incidentally, they gave me as meekly as though I had been invested with the authority of an autopsist or an undertaker, I resolved never to do so again. On each of the few subsequent occasions when similar requests were made I responded with pessimistic noises over the telephone and retired to the nearest tavern for an hour or so of beer and juke-box music.

What with one thing and another, not so very many weeks elapsed before the city editor of that era, who had the anguished look of a displaced sports writer, informed me that I was no longer a police reporter; I was to "come inside" to join the pool of general assignment reporters, from which one could expect to be selected to cover anything from the weekly tea of a women's sewing circle to the first flight to the moon—anything at all, except, as a rule, the activities of the Police Department.

That I would have nothing more to do with the Police Department sounded too good to be true, and it was.

During the ensuing months I wrote weather stories, obituaries, and accounts of speeches delivered at luncheons of the Baltimore Junior Association of Commerce; met Susan Watson, a member of the teaching staff of the Baltimore Museum of Art; toured New England with the Baltimore Symphony Orchestra (the article given most prominence was a report from Boston that a gunman had held up the orchestra's business manager in his hotel, taken several hundred dollars and immobilized him by making him remove his trousers); attended the coronation of Queen Shenandoah XXII in the Apple

Blossom Festival at Winchester, Virginia; accompanied Mayor Thomas D'Alesandro of Baltimore to Hagerstown, Maryland, where on a bicycle he raced against and defeated the local mayor riding a mule; learned how John A. Cypulski, caretaker of the Haunted House at Carlin's Park, felt about pressing the button that activated the compressor that caused jets of air to blow up women's skirts ("O.K."); celebrated National Cage Bird Week; received a fifteen-dollar raise, increasing my salary to sixty dollars a week; married Susan Watson; went on a Maryland House and Garden Pilgrimage; reported a poetry reading by E. E. Cummings (the article was written in free verse and was printed entirely, of course, in lower-case type); witnessed the meeting of Robert E. Lee IV and Major General Ulysses S. Grant III at Appomattox Court House (they were cool); mourned the passing of Baltimore's last burlesque theater (it reopened); described a dog's funeral; attended annual banquets of the Maryland Wine and Food Society and Alcoholics Anonymous, and tested the handicapping system of Thomas J. White, Jr., a distinguished Baltimore horse player, at Laurel Park, and found it wanting.

Early in this period the paper's drama critic, Donald Kirkley, having already seen *Oklahoma!* several times, had me assigned to review a revival of the show at Ford's Theatre; and thus, because reviews were invariably signed, I got my first Baltimore *Sun* by-line. It was a heart-stirring experience. I read the by-line and the review again and again, and imagined unknown readers' reactions to every phrase, every word. In my imagination, the reactions were not unfavorable; as a matter of fact, one of these imaginary readers, a man of discernment and influence, was kind enough to recommend the review for an imaginary Pulitzer Prize, which I imaginarily accepted with a modest but elegant little speech. *The Sun* nowadays, of course, has another, more fastidious drama critic, R. H. Gardner.

5

The Baltimore story that might have been the most fun to get published was, admittedly, shamefully artificial. It was suggested by a New York psychiatrist's statement on the subject of rubber masks. He had commented that these masks, which entirely enclosed the wearers' heads, had become popular because so many people were tired of their own identities and wanted to submerge them, temporarily at least, in fantastic disguises. Timid individuals, especially, were said to enjoy the illusion of irresponsibility, the sense of immunity against critical observation, the suspension of inhibitions. Furthermore, though the psychiatrist didn't discuss this aspect of their appeal, the masks offered opportunities for scaring the hell out of other people.

All sorts of bizarre witches, werewolves, vampires, and science-fiction monsters were available in the toyshops and drugstores. Donald Symington, the actor, lent me a mask which, in its quiet way, was the most horrible of all: it was the deeply wrinkled, pale, bloated

17

face of a bald old man whose life quite obviously had been one nasty incident after another. The texture of the skin was so realistic that across a room of ordinary size it appeared to be natural; at closer range it became apparent that it was quite unnatural. Something, certainly, was wrong. But you couldn't see just what; you might have suspected unsuccessful plastic surgery.

A telephone call to the chief inspector's office at Police Headquarters soon ascertained the fact that there was no local law against wearing masks in public. Edwin P. Young, Jr., the beloved city editor of that era, agreed that it would be interesting to test the psychiatrist's theory and at the same time to see how Baltimoreans would react to a masked man among them. A still photographer was assigned to the story; and, when we told the Sunpapers' television station, WMAR-TV, what we were going to do, a newsreel cameraman was added to the expedition. It was agreed that I should go ahead without them, to avoid giving the game away too early, and that they would find me at a prearranged rendezvous on my experimental stroll.

I was accompanied by a colleague, Jacob Hay V, who then wrote for the *Evening Sun*. (He later decided that this sort of job was a luxury he could no longer afford, and went the usual way of underpaid reporters, into public relations and writing for magazines.) A master theoretician on all sorts of absurdities, he was on this occasion my consultant on costume and deportment. Need one be reminded that Hay was a pioneer exponent of such classic japes as the upside-down bedroom for inebriates, the bathtub full of colorless jelly, and the tightly furled, very large conifer, wrapped as a gift, for enemies with small houses? Once opened, the tree suddenly filled the room it was in and required considerable athletic agility or hard sawing to remove it.

With his tweed pork pie hat worn slightly askew, his eyes blazing with Pennsylvania-Dutch craftiness behind deceptively normal spectacles, his great Edwardian black moustache alertly a-twitch, his trench coat of many flaps and buckles trailing open, his blackthorn shillelagh stabbing holes in the sidewalk, his purposeful Groucho stride extending his legs beyond comfort, he was a brave and reassuring figure that summer morning as we approached Baltimore's Pennsylvania Station. I was wearing an inconspicuous gray suit, carrying my paraphernalia in a suitcase, and beginning to wonder whether this whole enterprise was necessary.

The suitcase was unpacked and stowed in a locker, and the contents were rapidly taken into a lavatory cubicle.

"The train will be here in less than five minutes," Hay said, smiling the ruthless smile of a mad scientist. "Steady, the Buffs!" he cried, raising his stick like a sword. "God be with you, my boy," he concluded, ecclesiastically pursing his lips.

First, the mask. It seemed tighter than when I had tried it on before; the apertures for seeing and breathing seemed smaller. In the hot, small room, the suffocating smell of rubber reminded me of gas at the dentist's.

"Two minutes," a voice said. "I'll be waiting at Travelers Aid."

I donned a dark woolen muffler, to cover my neck where the rubber ended and skin began.

After that, the coat. It was a vile, translucent olive-green plastic oilskin.

Next, a black Homburg, for that slightly sinister appearance of high-level foreign diplomacy.

And finally, black gloves. The sky was blue and the sun was shining; it was apparent that the clothes had been chosen for concealment rather than to suit the weather.

I grabbed the small attaché case plastered with exotic labels (Hotel Borg, Reykjavik; Shepheard's, Cairo; Royal Victoria, Nassau, etc.), a souvenir of the RAF.

"That'll shake the bastards," Hay had muttered grimly, meaning everyone in town who conformed to conventional mores without protest.

I opened the lavatory door, recoiled incredulously from the horrible man in the mirror, and hurried toward the main concourse where I would be able to mingle with the throng of passengers arriving now from the north.

People rushed past the man in the mask apparently not noticing him. This indifference was at once disappointing and relaxing.

Anyway, I thought, it would not matter to me if anyone did stare at the mask disapprovingly. At that moment I realized with profound relief that disapproval or disgust or fear or hatred would be wholly unpersonal. The psychiatrist had been right; the sensation of anonymity was an agreeable one. I faced the immediate future—or rather I non-faced it—with placid enjoyment, wondering in a quite detached way not what would happen to me but what would happen to the mask.

A young woman sat engrossed in paperwork behind the counter of the Travelers Aid Society. Not looking up in response to my deferential cough, she said, in a casual manner, "Yes? What can I do for you?"

"I was hoping, my dear young lady," I said with silky villainy, "that you might be so kind as to direct me to a hotel in your city known as the Sheraton Belvedere." The Belvedere is one of Baltimore's principal hotels, a few blocks from the station.

I noticed that the tightness of the rubber, slightly constricting my jaws, caused me to speak more slowly than usual. The resulting manner seemed old-fashioned and courtly, hinting menace and unstable false teeth.

She looked up with the bright institutional smile of a nurse. The smile congealed, stiffened, and broke. Her eyes widened and glazed. Her mouth opened and no sounds came out. I restrained an impulse to lean over the counter and pat reassuringly one of her rigid hands; the touch of leather would undoubtedly have brought forth a scream. Instead, I smiled; but the mask, of course, did not. I lowered my voice to the gentlest pitch, and terrorized her all the more.

"The Sheraton Belvedere—its address," I kindly reminded her. "That's all I want from you, my dear."

Stuttering incoherently, she pointed vaguely in the direction of the main doors.

"But where is it?" I demanded, sharpening just a bit.

"It's. . . . Please. One minute. I'll look it up." She seemed to be reviving, remembering the traditions of her service. Numb fingers scrabbled aimlessly through the telephone directory. I did not want tears to fall, so, bowing a few inches, I doffed my hat, thanked her for her courtesy and bade her a good day.

Turning away from the counter, I saw Hay's pork pie above an open newspaper that was shaking with silent laughter, and I remembered for a moment that this weird experience was supposed to be amusing. He was leaning against the wall with his ankles crossed and looked about as inconspicuous as a private eye in a television melodrama. Folding the top of the paper downward until his glasses peered over it, he saw that I was watching him and he gestured urgently with a half-hidden finger, pointing across the stone floor to an immobile man some thirty yards away in the uniform of a railroad police officer. As I turned my head to look at this worthy, he abruptly turned around and walked briskly in the opposite direction.

Immediately I noted my second reaction. I felt power. I understood for the first time something of the allure of armed robbery for its own sake.

The taxicab dispatcher, who ordinarily solicited passengers, was uncharacteristically subdued as I passed the rank of cabs outside the station.

On the other side of Charles Street, Baltimore's main north-south thoroughfare and the city's most fashionable shopping street, there was another policeman, a municipal one. I felt that he was watching me. Not wanting to be stopped so soon (no pictures had been taken), I resisted the impulse to hurry. My pace was stately, suggesting, I hoped, high status, strength of will, and inexorability of purpose. The policeman showed no inclination to get any closer. Having let me go some twenty yards beyond him, he followed at my own speed, maintaining our relative positions as we proceeded slowly downhill. To test him, in the middle of the first block, I suddenly crossed the street; he crossed the opposite way. I stopped; he stopped. I went on; he went on. In a spirit of playful malice, I crossed back again at the end of the block; so did he. "That man," I said to myself, "is following me."

The mask and I looked around at him, and at Hay, and ahead once more, to see a short, fat man running toward me and winding a movie camera, and another photographer bearing the conventional black and silver Speed Graphic, that ubiquitous recorder of human disasters and buffoonery. The witnesses were assembled; it was time to make a few calls.

The first store specialized in women's underwear. After a momentary flutter, as in a disturbed dovecote, women in furs pretended studiously to examine the structure of brassieres. I said I wanted a corset.

"Yes, sir," said a bespectacled middle-aged saleswoman of armadillo-like compactness. "And what sort of foundation does madam require?"

It wasn't for madam, I said; it was for me, and I would like to be measured because of certain irregularities that required careful fitting. As my appearance penetrated her myopia, the saleswoman's hauteur diminished. She smiled hopelessly and in a nervous hand gathered the tight brown curls at the back of her crêpe neck. Her professional poise already lay about her in small fragments, like a broken Woolworth necklace. She was not without a certain pathetic appeal.

"I don't know," she said. "I'm sure we don't. . . . I don't quite see how. . . . I could ask."

"I never used to have this trouble in Berlin," I said. "But thank you, and a good day to you." I withdrew, wishing only that I might have been able to listen to the buzz of speculation that must have begun as the door swung shut behind me.

In a travel agency, the clerk was nudged close to the precipice of hysteria by a request for accommodation aboard the *Titanic*.

A girl in a drugstore fled into the pharmacy when I asked for a box of pancake makeup and a bottle of wig fixative. Through a pane of frosted glass I saw the blurred image of a man in a white coat picking up a telephone.

In a Chinese restaurant, an imperturbable Chinese waiter confronted me with polite obstinacy. They were not serving swallow's-nest soup, he said; and anyway, though appearances suggested the contrary, there were no unreserved tables that day.

I walked through the lobby of the Belvedere without incident, descended the stairs to the barbershop and asked whether Miss Parker, my usual barber, could give me a facial massage. The Negro shoeshine boy courageously barred my way to her end of the salon.

"Miss Parker, she ain't here, sir," he said. I saw that in fact she was.

"When will she be back?" I asked.

"She ain't goin' to *be* back," he said.

In the street I attempted to stop several people to engage them in conversation. Children were fascinated, but mothers were frightened. At last it began to occur to me that I might be exceeding the proper limits of journalistic enterprise. Far from amusing myself, I was now beginning to feel as though I had some conspicuous disease.

I was relieved of my isolation in Mount Vernon Place, near the Washington Monument, about half an hour after the experiment had begun. Two policemen, with hands on their revolvers, quickly converged on me from either side.

One of them stared closely into the mask and asked: "What you doing, wearing the false face?"

"Just trying it out," I replied.

"All right, don't get smart," said the other officer. "Take it off." While recognizing that the police in this instance actually represented the interests of society, my real identity began to assert itself, demanding protection against public exposure.

"I'd rather not take it off where I can be seen."

They flinched. For all they knew, there might have been something far more disgusting beneath the mask than the mask itself.

"You'd better come downtown with us," the first officer said.

"You mean I'm under arrest?" I said, translating the familiar police euphemism. As I recalled all the dreary evenings wasted in police stations, all the police humor I had endured, a spiteful impulse caused me to add: "What's the charge?" I looked forward to writing about policemen's ignorance of the laws of their own city.

"All right, let's go," said the second officer, seizing my elbow decisively, "you'll know what the charge is soon enough."

We stood stupidly for about twenty minutes beside a police call box on a street corner, waiting for the wagon, which had gone screaming off to a wrong address. A small crowd assembled. The public was no longer nervous about the mask. There was a good deal of scornful laughter—but it was directed against the police.

When the wagon arrived I was roughly hustled inside and the doors were slammed shut. I looked out through the steel mesh, but I couldn't see Hay. He had gone to telephone the paper. The wagon smelled of stale vomit. I felt tired and sad.

"We'll soon be where we're going," one of the officers said in a vaguely threatening voice.

As we bounced about on the wooden benches on the way to headquarters, I took off my hat and gloves and peeled off the hot rubber mask, which was dripping inside. The police looked cheated and angered by my untimely compliance.

They charged me with disorderly conduct. I didn't have twenty-five dollars to deposit as collateral, so a turnkey took me back to a cell.

The cell door banged shut; the turnkey's footsteps on concrete receded; the outer door banged; and, for a moment, there was silence.

"Psst—hey!" called a voice from the next cell. I got up from the wooden bench and stood near the bars.

"Yes?"

"What you in for, Mac?"

"I was wearing a rubber mask," I said.

There was a long, low, respectful whistle.

"Stick-up, huh? Tough break, fella."

There was a pause.

"Hey," said the voice. "How about doing me a favor?"

"What is it?"

"Tell me a job that's been pulled around here last Wednesday, some time in around there. I want to plead guilty to something. This broad up in Jersey says I had her locked up in a house up there, says I raped her. It looks bad, see, on account of she's only seventeen, the pig. D'you know any small jobs in Baltimore could of been pulled around that time?"

"Nothing small," I said.

"No," he said. "I guess you wouldn't, not in a mask."

Pause.

"Hey, do you have a cigarette?"

I couldn't give him even a cigarette.

There was silence again.

I had read a large number of the indecent inscriptions on the walls of my cell, and, though I had never before sympathized with mural graphomaniacs, I now began to understand them. I was on the point of reaching into my pocket for a copy pencil (its soft, black lead being ideal for graffiti), with the intention of noting a few home truths about the facilities and the management of the place, when I remembered that everyone arrested is supposed to be allowed to make one telephone call.

A few minutes of shouting and pounding and kicking were sufficient to attract the attention of the turnkey. Without much grumbling, he allowed me to call the city desk. It was shortly before payday, so nobody at the city desk, not even all of them combined, could raise the collateral. An expense voucher had to be signed by the managing editor and taken to the cashier. Eventually a fellow reporter, grinning from ear to ear, came and got me out. A magistrate's hearing was scheduled for later the same day.

The Sunpapers' lawyer and a senior political reporter were assigned respectively to conduct and observe my defense in court, and a few other members of the staff came along for the fun of it. But there wasn't much fun. The police and the magistrate were as succinct as possible. The magistrate, having checked a tome or two, ruled that I had not committed a misdemeanor, that wearing a mask did not constitute disorderly conduct, and that in view of the circumstances (I was a reporter, doing my job), taking all things into consideration (as a political appointee, he did not want to antagonize *The Sun*), he had decided he would dismiss the case.

The city editor and I were delighted with the pictures. Neil S. Swanson, the executive editor, was not. They shocked him. The movies and stills alike were scrapped. My story was spiked. Hay's account of the ludicrous adventure was restricted by order to a few flat paragraphs.

"*The Sun* reports news," Swanson said. "It does not make news." At the time, I thought his attitude on the matter was stuffy. Now I think that about this he was right. But I'm glad that he had not heard of the project before it could be executed. Altogether, the experience had been an educational, toughening one. After that, with increasing ease, I found that I could approach strangers and ask them preposterous questions. This process could be facilitated by knowing more about the rules than they did, and by wearing an imaginary mask of thick skin.

6

By the spring of 1951 I had been on *The Sun* for three and a half years, my duties remained unchanged, and my salary seemed to have got stuck somehow at $75 a week, which was barely enough to subsist on, and left next to nothing for the little niceties of life, such as paying the doctor's bills. Even apart from economic limitations, normal social activities would have been impossible because of my hours, from 2:30 to 11:30 P.M. There were two days off a week; but, because the paper was published every day, the holidays were just as likely to occur in the middle of the week as at the end.

I spent most of this time writing feature articles. One of them appeared almost every day, filling the space that was left between society news, drama criticism, the knitting pattern, the crossword puzzle, and answers to questions about etiquette and affairs of the heart, on the woman's page. This occupation was not arduous. Frivolity was encouraged. Time drifted by easily. There were countless interviews with all sorts of women, women librarians, women teachers, women strip teasers, even a woman pilot. They must have been strangely alike; seen in retrospect, the whole era is a blur that could be represented adequately in a movie by the pages of a calendar falling like autumn leaves. My wife would describe the period as drab; to me it was merely monotonous. Euphoria eluded us. I found it more and more difficult to achieve that air of insouciance and amiability that is a *sine qua non* for reporters who must stimulate ordinary people to chatter brightly about their unexciting lives. Even then, I believe, I was beginning to comprehend the terrible fact that wasting time amounts to committing suicide, slowly.

It was against this background of near-poverty, frustration, and self-pity, at a time when the biggest news was being made by soldiers in Korea, that one of the assistant city editors, with a wink and a nudge and a click of tongue against palate, informed me that I was a lucky guy, because Jane Russell, the movie actress, was to visit Baltimore, and I was to interview her.

The interview took place late the next morning, in the drawing room of her hotel suite. Two RKO Radio Pictures publicity men and two photographers were already there when I arrived.

Whisky and soda and the official studio biography were served while we waited for Miss Russell. The biography consisted of two or three mimeographed pages that briefly told the history of her life from birth in Minnesota to discovery by Howard Hughes and stardom in *The Outlaw*, the story of Billy the Kid. Jane was essentially a sensitive, introverted person, much given to critical self-examination, the studio said.

The door opened and she came in, wearing a black blouse, tight black velvet trousers, and a black scowl. She was snarling like a black panther with a migraine headache. She had not had enough sleep: she needed nine hours and she had had only seven. And didn't the goddamn hotel know how to make goddamn coffee?

"I'm dead until I've had coffee," she said.

Even after coffee the conversation was no better than it usually is in that sort of interview. We talked about Vincent Price's art collection and the sort of picture she'd like to make next and a new brand of nail-polish remover. While the photographers pleaded for a little more cleavage I looked through my few chaotic notes, inwardly groaned, and drank whisky.

She put on a mink coat and was driven to the Easter Seals headquarters to pose with children on crutches. She looked uneasy.

She changed into a dark blue satin dress to meet a lot more newspapermen and a member of some association of motion picture censors at a cocktail party in her hotel.

In this age of public relations and "deep selling," all kinds of people were giving parties for the press—shipbuilders and aircraft manufacturers, art museums and literary societies, jockey clubs and professional ball teams, building contractors, restaurant associations, and any number of patriotic, fraternal, philanthropic, and political organizations. But for ease of admission, plenitude of refreshments, and staying power, there were no parties that surpassed the press parties underwritten by the motion picture industry.

Advance notice of Jane Russell's party traveled fast around the newspaper grapevine:

"There's going to be a Rappaport party at the Belvedere."

"Free-loading?"

"Natch. Everything you want."

"Where?"

"Rose Room; 4:30 on. Tell Porter and Manchester."

"Right. Did you tell Goodspeed?"

"It was Goodspeed who told me."

As 4:30 came near, typewriter after typewriter fell silent in the news room; desk after desk was stealthily abandoned. Even a couple of editors, those who were unusually well connected with their staffs, glanced furtively at clocks and reached for their hats.

In the homes of newspapermen, in rundown town-house apartments and in the bright, shoddy bungalows of jerry-built new suburban developments, prematurely haggard young women in aprons broke dishes, slapped babies, and gnawed their knuckles, in the panic rush, the anguish and turmoil, of hasty preparation to join their husbands for recreation at somebody else's expense.

Most of the men and some of the women were intelligent enough to be aware of their degradation. It made them resent both the paper and their benefactors. The usual results were fierce rapacity at the bar, savagely cynical conversation, and as much sourness in their prose as the paper would tolerate. The paper had a condescending attitude toward show business, especially toward movies, so that the best parties often resulted in the most insulting publicity. But still the studios, the distributors, and the exhibitors persisted, operating on the long established theory that any publicity is good publicity. Their representatives extended glad hands and bared their teeth in broad smiles, though they knew they were disliked, and though they, in turn, disliked almost all their guests.

"Jane's fabulous," one of the hosts said as he welcomed the invited and the uninvited impartially, with sustained bonhomie. "Isn't Jane fabulous? You'll love Jane. Wait till you meet Jane. Go get a drink, then let me introduce you to Jane. Believe me, this Jane has it. Jane's really different; no kidding; I really mean it; I'm really being sincere when I say it. . . ."

But the majority of the guests, those who were not compelled to write anything, were impervious to all appeals. They went to the bar and stayed there in small groups, talking only to people they knew, until their faces darkened and swelled and swayed and nodded together in bunches like overblown red tulips.

The censor put his hand on Miss Russell's shoulder in a pseudo-paternal way and said:

"Between you and I, Jane, as far as I'm concerned personally, there's nothing objectionable about photos of—a healthy young woman like you. If we were considering only men of maturity and high intelligence, I'd say, 'Show *The Outlaw* just the way it was made originally!' But the thing is: dare we expose the youth of our state to such . . . ?" His glance fell, lingered for an instant, and returned to her face. "Censorship is a heavy responsibility," he said.

"Uhuh," Miss Russell said.

When he invited her to dinner she said she wished she could make it but she couldn't; she had promised a newspaperman an interview; she turned and pointed to me. I was the only reporter whose name she knew.

So I took her to hear Johnnie Sparrow play the tenor saxophone at a little Negro club called The Frolic.

29

The music was marvelous.

"When I can pat my foot to the music," Sparrow used to say, "I know that other folks can pat theirs."

The place was really swinging. Nobody asked for her autograph. But she had not been unnoticed; I was given no check.

The taxi fares and tips had left me with about five dollars in my pocket. I took her to a restaurant in Little Italy, the East Baltimore slum where the call girls, the B-girls, the Mafia, and the Mayor lived. I knew that the owner of the restaurant, a woman who looked like a Neapolitan Sophie Tucker, was susceptible to celebrities.

Fortunately, the gamble paid off. Dinner was on the house.

When we parted at the hotel Jane said that she had had a ball. I think she really had. My night on the town was for her a glimpse of the good, simple life.

7

The following winter, on a leave of absence from *The Sun*, Susan and I were in a Trans World Airlines Constellation high above the Rockies on our way to The Coast. In the movie industry one never flies to Los Angeles; one may sometimes fly to L.A., but usually to The Coast. The very phrase seemed permeated with the seductive smell of money.

All our expenses to, in, and back from Hollywood were being paid by Howard Hughes, who owned TWA, RKO, and Jane Russell's contract. We were to spend a couple of months in Hollywood while I gathered biographical material for a book on Jane.

And so there we were, landing at Los Angeles International Airport, being met by a man in California non-athletic sports clothes, and checking into a villa at the Garden of Allah, on Sunset Boulevard.

The villa was a small one, consisting of a bedroom, a bathroom, a drawing room with a dining alcove, and a kitchen. There were two telephones. Immediately after the bellboys had left we called some

friends in Baltimore to describe our surroundings, to tell them that
there was a desk, but that I did not intend to do any writing for
a few weeks; that there was a kitchen, but Susan was not going to
cook, and that when we looked outside we could see moonlight
through palm fronds.

I rang a local number that had been given to me, and Perry
Lieber, the publicity director of RKO, welcomed us to California.

"You're going to need an automobile," he said. "Why don't you
go pick yourself up one tomorrow morning?"

"Oh, I don't know," I said, the extent of our expense allowances
having been left uncertain in New York. "I thought we'd probably
use taxis."

"When the sun's out," he said, "it's kind of nice to have a convertible." I conceded the point. He gave me the name of a garage a
few blocks away where I could pick out a car of a color scheme that
pleased us, and, "of course," charge it to the RKO account.

"And come on over and see us on the lot when you get settled,
tomorrow afternoon some time, if you feel like it."

Susan and I walked along a narrow stone pathway through what
the Garden of Allah management said was like "a garden in Old
Spain," past the free-form swimming pool (a homesick Russian
ballerina was said to have had it built the shape of the Black Sea),
across a small terrace, into the main hotel building, through the dining room and into the bar. It was with a reverent sense of the history
of the place, with awareness that its reputation for dry martini cocktails dated back to the days of the desperate gaiety of F. Scott Fitzgerald, that we ordered two martinis.

"How do you like them?" solicitously inquired Rocky, the bartender, who had the appearance of a superannuated prize fighter and
the gravely concerned manner of a Savile Row tailor, "quite dry?"

"Very."

He poured chilled gin into chilled champagne glasses and mur-
mured over them, softly, once each, "Martini and Rossi."

We had read *The Day of the Locust*, by Nathanael West, and
some other works on Hollywood by writers who had professed to
despise it, yet who had succumbed to its peculiar charms, and the
drinks were strong, so it was not in the least surprising to see a blonde

in besequined sunglasses, ermine stole, cyclamen matador's trousers and high-heeled shoes mince hippily into the room leading by the hand a very short dwarf with a very large head. She sat on a stool at the bar; he climbed up the crossbars of an adjacent stool as nimbly as a sailor climbing up rigging, took his place beside her, and said, in a bass voice:

"The usual, baby? Two vodkas on the rocks—or how about two vodkas on Rocky?" The dwarf laughed until he coughed and choked, and his companion kindly shook him.

At midmorning we had breakfast on the terrace by the pool. Two unemployed extras were playing chess and sipping Bloody Marys in the sunshine. The dwarf, in a big Mexican straw sombrero and a tiny bikini, was lying on his stomach on the warm tiles reading the *Hollywood Reporter* while the blonde sat leaning over him and fondly anointed his muscular shoulders with lotion. A waiter told us that the dwarf currently was a great success as a Teddy bear in TV commercials. Sweet dance music was being piped through the tropical foliage. The orange juice and hot buttered toast and black coffee tasted good in the open air. The scene was idyllic. I dived enthusiastically into the clear turquoise pool and came up shuddering and almost breathless with cold. The chess players looked amused. It was as though I had taken a big bite at a beautiful apple made of wax: at that time of the year, the swimming pool wasn't for swimming in; it was scenery.

We chose a pale pistachio-green convertible with red leather seats and a continuous alternation of jazz and commercials on the radio. The manager of the garage told me where to get gasoline and oil by signing for them. We drove fifty miles up the coast and inland between vineyards and back at high speed with the top down and the radio loud. I thought elatedly I might buy sunglasses and a Hawaiian shirt. Susan suggested lunch. There was hardly any money in my pocket. We returned to the Garden of Allah, our magical oasis, and ate and drank, and signed the check.

After a nap, there was just enough time to drive over to RKO, on Gower Street, to shake hands with the publicity department and to meet the cashier.

"Give Pat a couple hundred, so he can have some spending money in his pocket over the weekend," Lieber said. "He'll be coming in again to see you the first of the week." I tried to look equally casual as I stuffed uncounted cash into my jacket.

"Good," I said. "Now, if you'll excuse me. . . . I promised Jane that I'd get in touch."

West along Sunset; North at the Beverly Hills Hotel; up a long, gently inclined avenue of palms like giant pineapples, of green lawns and large white houses; up a steeper winding road between the cool rock walls of a canyon; still climbing, across the peaks of broken hills, over, down, up again, and around a cliffside road called Round Valley Drive—one couldn't miss it, just as Jane had promised; the mailbox was adorned with a golden cutout of a quarterback about to throw a football, identified in neat letters as R. S. Waterfield, "Robert the Rifle," her husband.

From the road, the house was invisible, set back on a small ledge that fell away precipitously on three sides. The steep, narrow driveway, like the first ascent of a roller coaster, tilted the car back alarmingly. Above the sulphurous haze and the clamor of Los Angeles, Jane had achieved in a small estate the secure sequestration of a mountain fortress. And everyone to whom she gave her periodically altered telephone number was under oath to guard it with his life.

Two Doberman pinschers the size of ponies reared high against a steel mesh fence and barked in deep angry voices, then turned aside and ran in circles, ululating plaintively because they weren't being allowed to strip the flesh from my bones.

The house was two storeys high, and much wider than deep. Massive asymmetrical blocks were lightened by large sheets of green-tinted plate glass and softened at the edges by creeping bougainvillaea, bright magenta and mauve blossoms. The second-floor expanse of picture windows overlooked Van Nuys, her childhood home, in a broad valley, and beyond that a range of mountains. Jane's house was a mirador, an aerie.

A corpulent brown Buddha with complacent eyelids and a reticent smile sat next to a gong between a sheltered stairway and an open three-car garage. I was tempted to seize the padded mallet hanging beside the gong, and to beat it in the slow, portentous manner of

34

the athlete who identifies the productions of the J. Arthur Rank organization. Instead of doing this, however, I walked around one end of the house and up a ramp to the only door I could find. Feeling like a delivery boy, I made an effort, tightening the knot of my tie, to feel like a biographer.

I rang the bell.

"All right! All right! Come in!" screamed a voice, female, harsh, and impatient.

I was in a sewing room, a pantry, a nursery, an all-purpose room adjoining the kitchen, which could be seen through a doorless doorway.

Jane Russell, a personification of Hollywood sensuality, a national symbol of glamour, success, and affluence, was in a white shirt and blue jeans, arranging a baby's diaper. She appeared to be having some difficulty, as though trying to force a large bundle of laundry into a small bag. Her hair was hanging all over her face as she bent forward with the tip of her tongue between her lips, taking great care to insert a pin through the diaper, not through the baby.

"Oh, *you*," she said when she looked up. "I'd forgotten. Why come in the back way, for heaven's sake?"

"I thought—"

"Here, watch Tracy. I'll fix some coffee. Don't let her fall on the floor and bust her head." Jane hoisted her adopted daughter's rubber shorts and pulled down her dress, and left her lying on the table. I put a hand on each side of the fat body to keep it from rolling. A grandmotherly woman, the baby's nurse, came in.

"Who has my little Tracy?" she demanded in a joking-scolding manner. "She has been changed, I suppose?" I said she had, and Tracy was carried away in the nurse's strong, possessive arms.

It's difficult to ask a woman intimate questions about her life when she seems so preoccupied with affairs of domesticity. She was having trouble with a coffee percolator.

"I detest gadgets," Jane said. "Do you know anything about electricity?"

Once it was plugged in, the percolator began to work all right. I made a furtive note: "detests gadgets." Soon the potion was prepared that transformed her from female Hyde to female Jekyll. We went into the living room, a vast expansive room that suggested roller skates.

"What do you want to know," she asked.

"Well, everything," I said. "First of all, could you tell me. . . ." My voice faded anxiously as I heard heavy paws drumming in crescendo across the kitchen floor. The next moment, the two giant dogs, an avalanche of bone and muscle, burst into the room.

"Lie down, you idiots!" Jane told them. "They're quite insane," she said tolerantly as they raced around the chairs. One of the dogs suddenly ran straight at me. Unashamedly I raised a protective forearm across my face. But the dog only collapsed at my feet, all four of its legs wriggling feebly in the air, in the manner of a capsized insect.

"She wants to be petted night and day," Jane explained sympathetically.

We talked about dogs for a while.

"Would you like to see the rest of the house?" she asked, already leading the way.

The books in the library were revealing—*The Hunter's Encyclopaedia, The Dickens Digest, Success in Letter Writing, Chinese Household Furniture, Hollywood Album,* a few book-club novels, *Handbook of Athletic Games, Bartender's Guide,* the latest edition of the *Encyclopaedia Britannica, How To Tie Flies, Sexual Behavior of the Human Male, Fun in Bed, The Fireside Book of Dog Stories, Living the Creative Life, The Predicament of Evolution, The Greatest Story Ever Told, The Law of Faith,* and several other popular theological works.

The library was also Waterfield's den or lair. Here were his television set, rack of rifles and shotguns and boxes of ammunition, the stuffed pelts of a couple of animals he had killed, and trophies of his success as a professional football player.

Jane showed me their facilities for fine-weather entertaining, a harp-shaped pool, which could be illuminated from within so that it glowed at night like a giant aquamarine; a stone terrace, with a barbecue fireplace and, behind sliding doors, a bar, and the swimmers' changing rooms, with Jane Russell murals—nude Hawaiian girls on the walls of the men's room, and almost nude men on the walls of the women's room.

She showed me her purple dressing room, its built-in closets, her sixty pairs of shoes, her collection of slacks, her bathing suits and shorts, her evening gowns, her fifteen jackets and coats, her sweaters without number, her thirty-five pairs of earrings.

We were just leaving her bedroom as Waterfield entered the living room from the opposite end.

He was a hard, sun-tanned man in T-shirt and jeans. His head looked as though it had been carved hastily in teak with a blunt chisel. A bottle of beer protruded from his mouth. A rifle was slung over his left shoulder. He reminded me of Mickey Spillane as portrayed on the covers of some of his novels. Like Spillane, Waterfield looked as though at every indolent step he was ready to leap, dive, somersault, or otherwise go into violent action, hurling the bottle from his right hand and simultaneously firing from the left hip. His powerful neck and short-cropped hair gave the impression that he would never have to walk around anything he preferred to tunnel through. I found myself hoping that if the worst came to the worst his taxidermist would do a good job on me—perhaps I might be arranged in note-taking pose and identified with a small metal plaque as "Reporter."

But Waterfield was friendly, if not articulate.

"Hi, lovie," Jane said.

" 'lo, dear," he said.

After a few minutes, in which he and I desultorily discussed our belief that sunny days were finer than smoggy ones, Waterfield retired to watch television and Jane made tunafish sandwiches for lunch.

"Now what is it you really want to know?" she asked when she and I had settled again.

"Well," I said, "suppose you start by—"

There were cries from the baby's room. Jane looked around. The nurse came in bearing Tracy.

"She wants to play," said the nurse.

"O.K. Put her down here."

"Why not just start with the first things you can remember," I suggested eventually. "My earliest memory, for example, is being wheeled in a barrow in an apple orchard in Normandy."

"That's nothing," she said. "Dianetics took me back all the way. I can remember being in the womb. In the womb I was perfectly happy. I just lay there in the warmth and darkness. It was all mine. Nobody bothered me. I didn't have to do a thing.

"But then suddenly I felt sick to my stomach. I felt as though I was standing on my head. I had to push, push, push, until I felt as though my head was pushing my neck right into my body.

"I was born with a splitting headache. I was surrounded by all these *people!* They bored the hell out of me. I knew I'd really had it. I felt like saying, 'All right, you guys—leave me alone, will you?' But I knew they wouldn't.

"Tracy!" Jane yelled in protest, leaping and snatching from the baby a copy of *Silver Screen*, a movie fan magazine with a cover picture of Jane Russell. "Don't tear that, damn it! Here—" she handed Tracy a copy of *Screenland*—"tear Betty Grable."

8

I interviewed Russell Birdwell, the public relations man, who had done more than anybody else, except, perhaps, Howard Hughes himself, to make Jane Russell a well known star.

I took Birdwell to lunch. It was the first time that I had bought lunch for a publicity man; in the past they had always bought lunch for me. The reversal of the usual relationship was refreshing. All newspapers should fortify their reporters by enabling them to pick up at least their share of the checks in such circumstances. Reporters who are able to pay their own way don't sell out so readily; nor otherwise do they feel impelled to prove their resistance to blandishments by writing hypercritically.

"Building Jane Russell was three years of day and night work," Birdwell said. "We set up a thousand stunts. And when I say a thousand stunts, I mean a thousand stunts. We caused things to happen in Paris, France. We caused things to happen in London, England. All over the world things were erupting about this girl.

"There were heartaches, problems, difficulties to overcome. There

39

were complaints we were showing too much breast. We took that to court. We went prepared. We employed mathematics to figure out the skin area revealed by Jane in proportion to her size. We had 40-by 60-inch photos of Jane and other stars prepared. We were able to prove that Jane wasn't showing any more in proportion to what she had than any of the other stars were. Why should she be persecuted because she was better developed? We won the case."

Birdwell didn't take all the credit for the success of the publicity campaign. He acknowledged one of Howard Hughes's contributions.

"You know," Birdwell said, "Howard designed the brassiere Jane wore in *The Outlaw*, when other designers had tried and failed. Howard knows what he wants. He won't settle for less. He's a perfectionist. Nobody seemed to be able to get exactly the right uplift, the ideal separation we were striving for. So he got out his drawing board and went to work. He applied the principles of aeronautical engineering and made the best damn set of blueprints for a bra the world has ever known."

By the end of the Birdwell campaign for *The Outlaw*, the public was so conditioned, Birdwell claimed, that "they couldn't see anything round—doughnuts, cymbals, smoke rings, melons—without reacting: 'Jane Russell'! It was the greatest."

I interviewed a couple of writers who had written scripts for Jane, three directors who had directed her, her dress designer, hairdresser, make-up man, a cameraman and a still photographer, her personal publicity woman, Jane's friends, and her mother. Whenever I got the opportunity, I questioned Jane exhaustively, and got her opinions, on many subjects. The French Riviera: "Fabulous—just like Southern California"; Lucille Ball: "A living doll"; Gainsborough: "He stinks"; an Armenian dish consisting of spiced mincemeat wrapped in grape leaves: "Heaven"; Robert Mitchum: "A living doll." I felt as though I were gradually constructing Jane's portrait life-size, in two dimensions, like one of those big cardboard cutouts of movie stars in theater lobbies.

Jane spoke so admiringly, so often, of Mitchum that I went with her to the studio early one morning to meet him. When we arrived at the vast, somber, hangarlike building marked "Stage 11" Mitchum happened to be standing outside, getting some air between scenes. A tall, hefty man wearing combat boots and olive-green combat fatigues with silver eagles on the shoulders, he looked forlorn until he saw Jane. This was their first meeting since his return from several weeks on location in Colorado and her return from a month in Europe. She ran across the studio street squealing with joy.

"Mother!" he shouted, as she leaped into his arms. Arms around waists, chatting as animatedly as children, they ambled through the stage door and across a dusty concrete floor, through gray obscurity, toward the set. The place was eerie: the atmosphere was charged with the presence of many people, yet all of them were out of sight, and most of them were silent. The small sounds of cautious technicians were absorbed by insulation high overhead, above a Piranesi complexity of scaffolding and catwalks.

At last they walked beyond the dark row of mobile dressing cubicles and the unphotographable blank side of the scenery, and came to the bright center of things, part of a United Nations airground briefing room in Korea. Several U.N. Infantry and Air Force officers, mostly American, all smartly shaved and combed and starched and pressed and polished, were sitting alertly at tables near brilliantly illuminated wall maps and a blackboard on which someone had chalked clear but cryptic symbols presumably of tactical significance. The officers' faces had the smooth, healthy, contented, inhuman appearance of faces in a recruiting poster. Four carpenters were quietly playing cards on an upturned packing case. The director was making annotations on his script. A cameraman was tape-measuring the distance from a window to the lens of the camera. A couple of electricians were adjusting the spotlights and wire mesh screens diffusing the illumination of a photographic panorama of Korean houses, the view from the window.

"O.K.!" the assistant director shouted, clapping his hands imperiously. He had just seen Mitchum come in. "Here he is. Let's have some quiet now! Let's get on the ball! Let's go!" Murmurous conversations stopped.

"I've got to go and recite," Mitchum apologized to Jane. "Put it down here a minute." He patted a camp stool at the periphery of the entanglement of electrical equipment. "This won't take long."

A man with blue stubble on his beefy jowls and an unlighted cigar between his teeth hurried to Mitchum and touched his forehead and cheeks with an orange powder puff. This cosmetician, the head make-up man on the lot, known as Shotgun, was shared by Mitchum and Jane. Submitting to the powder puff, Mitchum slumped his shoulders forward and distended his stomach in the posture of the Sad Sack. Shotgun produced a comb and deftly arranged Mitchum's forelock in romantic disarray. In this movie, as usual, Mitchum was supposed to be conspicuously active. He pressed his hands between his knees and pivoted coyly away, like the shy young girl bather in "September Morn." Shotgun patiently chewed his cigar and dulled Mitchum's nose with more powder.

"Well, suh," Mitchum said, assuming his hardy Kentucky drawl, "I reckon it's time we-all got back to war." Turning toward Jane for a moment, he added, "There's a jug of sake a-bubblin' on the hot plate in my dressing room, in case you-all feel in the mood for refreshment."

Jane shook her head and clicked her tongue in mock despair. "Isn't he hopeless?" she asked me. "Isn't he divine?"

Mitchum was earnestly singing "Mammy's Little Baby Loves Short'nin' Bread," while his fellow players desperately muttered their lines to themselves before the call for action.

An electric bell rang. There was dead silence, except for the last few words of "Mammy's Little Baby." The assistant director hissed, "Shh! Please!" and cried, "Quiet now, everybody!" The director said, "All right, roll 'em!" And the camera was running.

"The South Koreans have come a long way since the Commies first jumped," Mitchum said. "They're really armed and trained now." He walked with an easy, slow swagger through the other officers, and led them to the window to look out.

"Cut!" ordered the director. "Bob," he said in an unnaturally calm voice, "you put your hand through the window again." This gesture weakened the illusion of reality, because the window was shut and there was supposed to be glass in the frame. The panes had to be imaginary to avoid reflections.

"I did do it again, didn't I?" Mitchum said. In a loud, hoarse, melodramatic aside, he added: "Better had I been a procurer."

The brief passage of monologue and the simple action were tried again and again, and finally were accepted.

"And do you realize, gentlemen," said another officer ardently, "this'll definitely put us on the offensive?" There were authentic grimness and weariness in Mitchum's voice when he responded: "Don't you think it's about time?"

It suddenly occurred to me that Mitchum was feeling rather embarrassed playing the part of a hero in the Korean War in a second-rate movie while other men of lesser physiques were still involved in the real thing. On a subsequent occasion, drinking stingers from tumblers and listening to Joe Bushkin playing the blues at the Hangover Club at three o'clock in the morning, Mitchum said he was deeply dissatisfied with his work, but, whether I believed it or not, he needed the money; he had got into hock at the time of his arrest for marijuana. "But, hell, what are *you* doing?" he asked me. I was a reporter, and I wasn't in Korea either.

During another break in the shooting, Mitchum rejoined Jane.

"Tell me what happened in Colorado," she suggested. "I hear you've been brawling in bars again."

"Yes, Jane," he said with dignity. "There was an incident. It occurred in a public place of refreshment. The guy was shwacked; but shwacked, Jane.

"I am standing talking to a colonel—a *real* colonel—when I notice this character, this private, giving me dirty looks. 'I can lick that son of a bitch,' he says." Mitchum indifferently shrugged his massive shoulders. "O.K., O.K. This can be ignored. The joint is crowded. I don't want to make any trouble. Somebody says this guy is the heavyweight champion of somewhere. So what am I supposed to say? Then he comes up too close, and the colonel says: 'Fix your necktie, soldier.' He is a very sloppy soldier. He gives the colonel a shove in the chest. You can see the colonel doesn't like this. Already the private can be put under arrest. The colonel is more patient than I am.

"I grab the guy and shake him a little and say, 'Now listen, Jack: straighten up, will you?' I bang his head against the wall a bit, to show I'm serious. He won't listen to reason. He starts swinging." Mitchum rolled his eyes upward in sham horror, drew in his naturally receding, but solid, cleft chin, turned his head to one side and covered

43

himself with upraised hands, palms fore. "Gee, don't strike the fair princess! I get him by the lapels and bang his head on a table for a while. 'Cut it out, Jack,' I say, trying to soothe him, 'or else someone may get hurt.' Someone calls to have me pulled off." Mitchum looked aghast; reformers are so often misunderstood. He reminiscently felt the back of his thick neck. "This can become serious. Now I have a thumb in his eye; but he is getting hysterical. A very excitable character. So a couple of guys pull me, and I pull, and I notice that my friend is not fighting; he is lying on the floor. This is some champion. So I raise my foot, a slow upswing. Some prude says: 'Now don't you kick him!' He says this to me, the protector of the peace. Well, I do just bounce a little one off his bonnet, just for luck. They take him to the hospital; there is nothing broken. Then all the newspapers. While you were a kidnaper, Jane, adopting the Irish boy, I was a murderer. Sometimes reporters make me want to throw up. Did I or did I not hit the guy? Sure I hit him. But he was the one who was out of line. I had to talk to the colonel so the soldier didn't get sent to the stockade."

"Everybody wants to slug Tarzan," Jane commented. "Everybody wants to beat up Bogie, and Vic Mature, and Kirk Douglas. Everybody wants to prove he's tougher than Mitch."

"It isn't fair," Mitchum agreed equably. "So let's get loaded."

The next morning, when I went to see Mitchum alone, to ask him some questions about Jane, he was in his dressing room in his tropical sun-tan dress uniform decorated with the French *croix de guerre* and palms.

"Today," he said, "I'm on leave. In Japan? I don't know. Japan, Korea—what's the difference? Anyway, you're in time for breakfast."

A beaker of light amber fluid was fuming sweetly on the hot plate.

"Have some sake," he suggested.

He was eating sardines and overripe Limburger cheese that was liquefying with putrefaction and shockingly pungent.

"I'm scheduled to make love this morning," he said with disgust. "If there's anything I hate it's making love on an empty stomach."

After winning his leading lady's hand in marriage, Mitchum came back to his dressing room and complained to his secretary that it smelled like the burning ghats of the Ganges.

"When you're in Beverly Hills, get some incense, for God's sake."

"Incense," she acknowledged.

"Make it jasmine," he said.

"Right. There's Scotch in the cupboard and plenty of ice."

"That girl's a genius," he said to me. "Now how did she know that I want to get good and *dronk?*

"She's a good kid," Mitchum said, as his secretary left the room and he began making drinks. "I like her. But you want to talk about Jane. Here is a living legend in the tradition of Lillian Russell and Mae West. They have in Jane a great hunk of beautiful, healthy protoplasm. What do they do with her? They have her behave like a block of wood. And yet Jane is really a very intelligent dame.

"Ain't everything ridiculous though? Pour another drink. You say you're going to write about Jane. I don't see how it can be done; she's usually in hiding, and not only when she's in public. I wrote a book once, a novel. I don't know what happened to it. Before that I drove trucks. Writing, driving, acting—what's the difference? I'll tell you one thing: playing colonel out there is the easiest way I know to get the dough to pay for Scotch like this. It's twenty years old, man."

After a certain time, he began singing softly bebop, and drumming expertly with his fingertips on a coffee table.

"Let's cut out," he said. "We've only a few hours to get in the mood to go listen to some jazz."

9

As my waist fattened and as bringing pen to paper became increasingly difficult, except to sign checks, I began to notice with misgivings what sort of writing was being done by reporters on the staffs of Los Angeles newspapers.

Apart from stories about the occasional torrential rains that sent cascades of liquid mud down the canyons and flooded the valleys, the big news appeared under headlines such as these: "LILI DENIES SHE WAS NUDE," "JOAN BENNETT MATE JAILED" and "TONE-PAYTON PFFFT!"

The editorial emphasis was at best bizarre. The style was tawdry. I couldn't judge the accuracy of the reporting, except in one instance that affected me. A short item by Mike Connolly, a columnist in *The Hollywood Reporter*, was more wrong than right. Connolly reported: "RKO brought Pat Catlin out from NY to write a biog on Jane Russell, to be published some time next year. Studio's paying him $1,000 a week." He had got the name wrong; I hadn't come from New York; the book was not scheduled for publication the following year; and the studio had not fixed the level of weekly payments.

I met some other columnists and correspondents of several nationalities. They had an expensive, massaged look about them; their costumes were more impressive than their conversations.

"It's fabulous here at Christmastime, the number of presents we get," said the representative of a London tabloid. "Some of these people must spend thousands: they give gold cigarette cases, monogrammed silk shirts, cases of booze—the lot. You've never seen anything like it. And you realize, don't you, that the landscape and climate of southern California are a lot more like the Holy Land's than all that snow and holly routine?"

Susan and I spent our loneliest Christmas in Hollywood. We sent even more cards than usual; we received fewer, as though some friends had felt that we were beyond communication. We were not consoled by the pink metallic Christmas trees along Hollywood Boulevard.

We attended an informal house-warming. The exterior of the building was orthodox, with the conventional patio and swimming pool; the inside was not so orthodox. The living room was a dream-jungle: gnarled tropical trees festooned with flowering creepers were wedged between ceiling and floor. The blossoms were orchids, tied on. Numerous guests were milling about in the dim light, helping the overworked bartenders by helping themselves. Nobody seemed to know why he was there. Nobody seemed to know the identity of the host. Susan, wanting water, took a glass to a row of faucets behind the bar. The first one gushed bourbon; the second, Scotch; the third, champagne. She tried the kitchen, but soon returned and reported: "It's no use. The water's rusty."

Almost every day we drove by the Hollywood Mortuary, which was across Sunset Boulevard from LaRue, the scene of a celebrated underworld shooting. The mortuary was most notable for the great clock above the front doors. The dial was clearly marked with Roman numerals; and, ordinarily, a long pendulum swung to and fro with the slow, deliberate regularity of an old man swinging a scythe; but there were no hands marking the time of day—the sort of deficiency in a clock that makes one a bit uneasy. Jane's theory about the handlessness was that the dead, being in eternity, were beyond time. En route to Beverly Hills one day I noticed with a tightening scalp that the pendulum had stopped, slightly off plumb. I went in to inquire about it.

A man in blacks and grays with a white boutonnière rose to his feet behind the reception desk, his hands clasped, his face composed in an expression of sympathetic grief and quiet courage. Questioned about the clock, he relaxed and said that its having no hands simply signified that the mortuary would answer a call day or night: " '24-hour service' "—he was quoting the sign outside, which lit up blue after dark. The arrest of the pendulum had been accidental; it was to be repaired as soon as possible, he said.

Considering mortality and remembering *The Loved One*, by Evelyn Waugh, we drove to Forest Lawn Memorial Park, and heard a lecture on "the world's largest religious painting," an oil by Jan Styka depicting Calvary. It measured 195 by 45 feet. After the lecture, we sat in the "Mystery of Life Garden," reading a brochure that said: "Beauty costs money, and the general development of Forest Lawn is no exception . . . [but] truly the dollar has greater purchasing value at Forest Lawn than anywhere else." That day I came to realize that Waugh was a more literal reporter, a less fanciful satirist, than I had previously believed. It was worth having gone to Hollywood to learn just that; the knowledge was encouraging; it made reporting seem more important.

Jane told me about The Sportsmen's Restaurant, where guests were given fishing tackle. I stood on a small bridge and fished for trout in a floodlighted artificial lake. The water was so full of fishes that they were flopping about, gasping; but I couldn't catch one. I dined on turkey, and asked myself whether my luck was running out.

Over eggs Benedict at the Brown Derby, Jane told me her ideas about what happens to one after death. She said she believed in eternal individual consciousness in a universe "which is to the world as the world is to an ant hill." One would survive for ever, fixed permanently at one's favorite age and "in perfect physical condition." I imagined Jane looking for all time as she looked that morning,

48

radiantly optimistic, breathing deeply in a violet cashmere sweater. She expected to spend eternity practicing interior decoration in some ideal, never-ending, outer-galactic, California-style housing estate.

It was just as well to clarify one's thoughts about life after death, she added, because she was quite certain that the end of the world that we knew would come "in our lifetimes," perhaps quite soon, "so we'd better be ready for it"; the final atomic holocaust was plainly foretold in the Old Testament. "Why don't you come to the Chapel tonight?" she suggested. "We always have a ball." I accepted with the alacrity of somebody buying his first accident insurance. It seemed fitting that Aldous Huxley was browsing in the Beverly Hills bookshop at which I called on the way to the Garden of Allah to change my clothes. To my account of the day's expenditures I added: "Holy Bible—$7.50," and looked uneasily over my shoulder, and wondered when the first punitive thunderbolt would come crashing in through the thin stucco walls.

The Chapel was a small building that Jane and her brothers had built beside their mother's house in the San Fernando Valley. Mrs. Russell frequently preached a fundamentalist doctrine of her own at informal evening services. Jane managed to get there two or three times a week. She often brought friends from Hollywood. Some of them were most inclined to go there for the first time when they were suffering from alcoholic or postmatrimonial remorse; a few of them returned again and again. Her recent converts included one of Bob Hope's directors and a musical arranger from Paramount.

That night, after the hearty singing of some old-fashioned hymns and the presentation of a comfortingly homely homily from the pulpit, the small congregation, a dozen young men and women or so, settled down on cushions on the floor while Mrs. Russell with unexpected fervor exhorted them to allow "the holy spirit" to use their voices. As Jane explained, if one could completely relax one's personality in humility, one might receive the gift of tongues; one might be able to serve as a medium for the words of God.

After only a few minutes of concentration, Jane, herself, was blissfully rapt. When she spoke, her voice was still what Mitchum had described affectionately as "that awful Van Nuys whine," but the

49

words were strange. An incomprehensible babble evolved into an Oriental singsong that was equally incomprehensible to me but suggestive of actual language.

Afterward, Jane told me: "When I get tongues it's usually medieval Chinese."

Sometimes sympathetic members of the congregation, though they knew no Chinese, were enabled to interpret what she said. Jane's manner was as casual as though nothing unusual had happened. "I'm starving," she said. "I'll fix coffee and cookies." Pausing on the way to the chapel kitchen, Jane laid a kind hand on a novice, a pretty little blonde who wanted very much to break into the motion picture industry, who was writhing about on a rug and agitatedly sobbing: "It won't come! I can't! I can't! I can't . . . !"

"Take it easy," Jane said. "You'll make it."

If I had taken it easy, I just might, I suppose, have been able to produce a manuscript that honestly recorded what I had observed in Hollywood, and that would also have gratified RKO, and a sophisticated New York publisher, and Jane Russell, and me. But I strained, and compromised, and failed.

Susan had to fly back to Baltimore to prepare to have a baby, our first. I spent a few days in Palm Springs and Las Vegas. I met a Texas oil man whose wife's poodle was undergoing psychoanalysis. I got back to Baltimore the day Sheila was born. She was normal. Normality was inspiring. I quickly finished a book—for children. I sent Jane a copy, and she said she liked it. She never reproached me as the months went by and it became evident that the book I had written about her was doomed to oblivion. We still exchange Christmas cards.

By the time I returned to the Baltimore *Sun* the Hollywood suntan had faded almost entirely away.

10

We accustomed ourselves to plainness and moderation, to the medium hues of life without persiflage and conspicuous waste. But Hollywood, for all its sham, perhaps because of it, had spoiled me for the dull periods of general assignment reporting. And the dull periods of reporting in Baltimore in summertime can be numerous, almost continuous.

My only memorable assignment in the summer of 1952 was to go to New York to find out whether it was true that the State Department had taken action to prevent Owen Lattimore, of the Johns Hopkins University, from traveling abroad. Senator McCarthy, without justification, had accused Lattimore of being a Soviet agent. I was able to substantiate our tip, and thus I achieved the one recognized, clear-cut news beat of my career. The executive editor gave me a bonus of two hundred dollars. Lattimore was not so grateful: he said he hadn't wanted to travel abroad anyway. But *The Sun* had struck a small blow for liberty whether Lattimore had the grace to acknowledge it or not. Nowadays, of course, he is as free as any other U.S. citizen in good standing to use a passport.

Summer in Baltimore had reached its final stage and the inmates of the city were deep in torpor when Dorsey, the managing editor, summoned me into his private office. When he withdrew from the news room into his inner sanctum and a reporter was sent in after him the odds were better than even that the reporter was in for an upbraiding. Dorsey was no martinet; however, he did take exception to reporters drinking gin in the photographic laboratory, getting drunk and hitting copyreaders, and committing other peccadilloes of the sort that has been associated romantically with the Chicago school of journalism memorialized in *The Front Page*, but which has not been exclusively limited to it, and which still manifests itself from time to time in even the most decorous newspaper offices. Perhaps because my own conscience was not altogether clear, I approached Dorsey's office with some trepidation, in the manner of an English schoolboy approaching the dark, dreadful study of his headmaster. I had metaphorical exercise books stuffed into the seat of my trousers in preparation for the metaphorical caning that seemed almost inevitable, although on this occasion, as I uneasily searched through the débris of recent memories, I could find no trace of any major dereliction.

"There's an Air Force junket to some new base in northern Greenland," Dorsey said, his face composed in that mask of rigid sternness that subsequently I learned to associate with his acts of kindliest beneficence. "You may as well go along."

It was difficult to realize that it had been this same managing editor, not so very long before, after I had spent a mere $120 on a three-day trip to western Maryland and Virginia, who had written a memorandum notifying the city editor that "out-of-town coverage by Mr. Catling is a luxury that *The Sun* can no longer afford."

If he had said, "Here's a million dollars; you may as well spend it," I could not possibly have felt any happier than I felt at that moment, having received my first foreign assignment.

It was Dorsey's policy when giving a foreign assignment to leave it quite nebulous, without any specific instructions about exactly where one was to go, how one was to get there, what one was to do, how long one was to stay, the amount of one's budget, and what one was to write. It was a good policy in many ways, I think, because it is practically impossible to foresee the way a story may develop; however, such unconfined freedom, suddenly conferred, can give a beginner sleepless nights.

With some fellow reporters I had often scoffed at what we regarded as the shortcomings of the paper's correspondents abroad. In the home office, it is not too difficult almost any day to decide how a correspondent might have been most usefully employed in the field the day before. In the home office, one wonders what on earth induced him to act otherwise. But now, about to go out on a story myself, I was already wondering how I would know what to write in the mysterious days ahead. For that matter, how did one compose a cable? What was cablese? Did one have to know a *lot* of Latin? And how could one think about style while thinking about the cost of semicolons? Nobody had said anything about how long the stories should be or how they were to be conveyed from Greenland to Baltimore.

By questioning men in the office who had been around, I pieced together an idea of what I needed and what I must do. It's wonderful how the secret lore of journalism, the practical knowledge beyond journalism schools, is transferred from generation to generation. During the next few days, I learned that it was essential to take a Hermes portable typewriter and a spare ribbon, copy paper, carbon paper, pencils, a penknife (with an attachment for opening bottles), *Roget's Thesaurus*, *Webster's Dictionary*, bilingual dictionaries and phrase books of the countries through which I would be traveling, Fowler's *English Usage*, Mencken's *American Language* (all of it), relevant issues of the *National Geographic Magazine* and maps, a dinner jacket, golf shoes and swimming trunks, a tape recorder ("vital for proving the veracity of quotations in case of being sued"), a miniature camera for photographing secret documents, credit cards for the world's major cable companies and airlines, an international medical certificate (bearing up-to-date stamps indicating the receipt of shots for smallpox, diphtheria, yellow fever, beriberi, sleeping sickness, blackwater fever, and yaws), letters of introduction to government leaders and diplomatic representatives in all appropriate foreign countries, a first-aid kit (including, among other things, sleeping tablets, stay-

53

awake pills, morphine, prophylactic ointments and lethal capsules for use when threatened with torture by secret police), a small automatic pistol, a money belt, a pocket compass, an American flag, an assortment of gaudy trinkets with which to appease aboriginal savages, a box of K rations, a box of Kleenex, and a bottle of Maryland rye whisky.

I had not as yet had the good fortune to meet Fred Sparks, an itinerant columnist, whose cardinal rules of foreign correspondence would have done much to allay my anticipatory qualms.

"As long as you know what country you're in and what day it is," he pointed out on a later occasion, "you've got it made. It's the dateline that's important."

I might have been encouraged as much by meeting Anthony Carson then, instead of years afterward in England. He said it was his practice as a free-lance writer, on his irregular excursions from London, to take with him only a cardboard suitcase full of dirty laundry, and a wallet containing evasive letters from editors, a few pounds sterling and a one-way, second-class railway ticket to a provincial city in a European country that was no longer, or not yet, fashionable. Apparently, the scantiness of his preparations suited his temperament; uncertainty was a stimulant: unknown and knowing nobody at the obscure terminus of his train ride, he set off from England with a fresh, almost an innocent, sense of novelty and infinite possibility. The rail terminus was always the beginning of an unmapped, unconsidered Odyssey, directed by accidental human encounters, leading to unimaginable situations in unexpected palaces, *pensions*, and youth hostels. Weeks or months after his departure, he would grope his way back to London with the wrong raincoat and a worn smile and material for some of the most desperately comic, realistically muddled, poetically allusive periodical literature of our time, and sometimes books as well.

But inspirational examples of this magnitude were beyond my immediate ken. I took what advice I could get.

One Pulitzer Prize-winner in the office said: "Take plenty of money. It's impossible to have too much. It doesn't make any difference whether you take it in travelers' checks or in cash. In either event, take it in small denominations, in tens and twenties, and don't change too much of it into foreign currencies at one time. To have too much foreign currency can be awkward when government officials abroad get angry. You must always be free to get angry back at them—prepared for deportation, in other words. By the way, where are you going?"

"Greenland," I said, as modestly as possible.

"Oh," he said, turning back to his typewriter.

"To see the new air base at Thule," I added.

"Yes," he said, without looking back. "Well," he concluded kindly, "I don't suppose you'll need much of anything there."

11

There were twenty-four of us, representing the major American and Danish news services, newspapers, magazines, and radio and television. The Danes had been invited because Greenland, after all, was a Danish possession; American bases had been established there in accordance with a NATO agreement.

We were flown north from an airport near Washington in a VIP aircraft with four engines and comfortable seats that tipped back like the seats in a superior bus. We seemed like a party of tourists. As soon as we were airborne, some of us began taking snapshots out of the windows; some played cards; some read books about the sights we were going to see; some wrote home; and some curled up in uncomfortable postures with their hats over their faces and slept.

The other correspondents—I had privately promoted myself from reporter to correspondent on leaving the city limits of Baltimore—were rather disappointingly unimpressive to look at. They were older than I; most of them were middle-aged, with spectacles and bald spots and an air of mortgages and unpaid bills which the jollity of the outing had only partially dispelled. Looking about me, I suspected that this cherished assignment might not be quite so important as I had presumed. Later, however, when we were flattered and coddled by a few Air Force generals, my self-esteem increased again.

As the first impression of homogeneity faded and separate identities emerged from the group, it became apparent that some of my colleagues were indeed knowledgeable, industrious and, in their special ways, distinguished men. The technical discourses between the *New York Times* and the *Herald Tribune* seemed so subtly politically significant, with hints of hidden scandal and possible congressional investigations, that I began to feel that regarding Thule as only an air base must be an obvious indication of the naïveté of my novitiate.

We landed in Massachusetts and Labrador for fuel, food, GI Arctic clothing, and briefings. A press briefing is a one-sided press conference in which experts impart prepared information and hand out written releases that give a favorable account of the presiding organization's part in the story being covered. In a high-class briefing, large, multicolored wall maps and charts are unrolled, slides are projected, pointers are used, and statistics are recited as persuasively as in a pseudoscientific television commercial. When the Air Force goes all out in this way, majors introduce colonels and the colonels introduce generals and the generals address the audience as "gentlemen" and read aloud what the majors' staff have written for them. For the listeners, who have already been given large Manila envelopes containing the mimeographic gist, or the text, or even an elaboration of what the generals read, the experience can be a debilitating one. There's not much for reporters to do except to try to think up impressive questions.

We were told that Air Force C-124's, C-97's and C-54's in all seasons of the past 17 months had flown 2,100 round trips to Thule, carrying 12,500 short tons of cargo and civilian and service personnel (men) without losing a single plane. And we were told a lot more along the same lines. Eventually, a major brightly announced that time was up and that each and every one of us was invited to attend a reception at the officers' club.

The next morning, with slight headaches, we left Goose, crossed the northern limit of wooded country, left Labrador, and flew over broad Davis Strait and up the coast of Greenland.

Colonel Bernt Balchen, USAF, a merry, plump, ruddy-cheeked Norwegian-American who looked like a smooth-shaven Santa Claus, had been assigned to our brief expedition as a guide and commentator. Reputed to know more about the Arctic than any other man, he said he believed it to be "the center of the civilized world today, in the air age."

Below us were the deeply crevassed edges of the great Greenland icecap, light-gray snow and dark-gray mountainous rock, and light-gray glacial ice imperceptibly moving down steep valleys into the dark sea. There were names on the map—Akunaq, Ujarasugssuk, Upernavik, Tuqtoqortoq, and others. There were villages down there. But I saw none. I saw nothing human, nothing animal, nothing vegetable. I saw nothing but the sea, and bay after bay, fjord after fjord, icebergs and glaciers, and the mountains and the icecap and the sky. The plane in which we flew was the only disturbance.

We cut across Melville Bay, passed Cape York, and rounded a hill and some red-lighted masts; and soon the wheels squawked on the runway. Arriving at Thule was, like the end of most spectacular flights, anticlimactically normal. Though the wind was like cold razor blades, it was difficult to believe that we were only 900 miles from the Pole and 1,500 miles from another base where visitors probably were gathering material for articles intended to encourage the readers of *Pravda* and *Izvestia*.

In the Thule Air Base officers' club the sense of familiarity was almost stupefying. Marilyn Monroe in the nude was spreadeagled on the wall behind the bar.

"There's one thing that's different here," a pilot said. "The ice in the highballs is thousands of years old. It's been under tremendous pressure." He held forward his glass. "Listen to that son-of-a-bitch crackle!" The drink made tiny noises like those emitted by a bowl of Rice Krispies.

After the tour of the base was over we sat at our typewriters and wrote long condensations of what we had been told. We might not have been able to write much more than we could have written in Washington (a censor who had flown up with us made quite sure of that); but we wrote with more enthusiasm than if we hadn't made the trip. We now had vested interests in the importance of the story: we had flown all that way; it had to be important.

The work having been done, the Air Force offered rewards, a flight over the North Pole and a visit to the Eskimo village of Thule, the northernmost self-sustaining settlement in the world. The flight over the Pole was nothing to write home about; once you've seen one ice floe you've seen them all. The visit to Thule was something special. The Danes did not customarily allow anyone to visit the village, for fear that it might be contaminated by the diseases and economics of the modern world.

Although he continued to wear his Air Force uniform, Colonel Balchen sighed as gratefully as a fat woman removing a corset when he left the confines of Thule Air Base and led the way to the small gray boats that were to take us the first part of the way.

Wolstenholme Fjord was misty. Blue ice islands with overhanging white cliffs floated near us in the smooth dark-green water. The putt-putt of the engine was the only sound. Nobody talked.

We were led past a small Danish settlement, over a rocky hill, toward the ancient Eskimo village. On the way there was a cemetery. Because of the hardness of the ground, the bodies had been laid out on the surface and covered with stones. There were a few crude wooden crosses and a faded cloth wreath decorated with embroidered flowers. I shuddered inside my hooded parka as I contemplated the loneliness of an uncovered grave on a barren hill in the cold mists of Thule, and compared this with the orderly suburban encampments of marble, granite, grass, and shrubbery under the supervision of gardeners, undertakers, and ministers in the crowded burial places of temperate lands. Death in Thule was only thinly disguised.

Staring at the rocky ground, I saw that it was not entirely lifeless. Accustomed to grosser vegetation, I had at first failed to notice the minute specks and blotches of rust-orange and -red funguses and withered brown lichen that clung to the stones. Beauty existed on the miniature scale of wild birds' eggs.

The Eskimo village was situated on miraculous turf, like peat, sloping down to the water's edge.

"This is the garden spot of the Arctic," Colonel Balchen said without irony.

We had expected igloos. But the Eskimos construct ice-block shelters only on hunting trips away from home. The huts at Thule were made of imported wood, fortified and insulated with layers of sod. Seen from outside, they looked like compost heaps.

We visited the most important man in the village, who was one of Admiral Peary's guides to the North Pole in 1909. His name was Odaq, which means "the seal lying on the ice." His age was unknown. His long black hair was still blue-black, cut in an exact fringe like a doll's wig. His round leather face was intricately wrinkled. His eyes were slits and his nose was flat. He had been warned that we were coming. When we bent our heads and entered his low-ceilinged room, he was sitting on the bed dressed in his best clothes: white sealskin boots, polar-bear-skin trousers, a white pullover and a dark blue woolen cap. From his chest dangled the red and white ribbon and the silver Distinguished Service Medal that had been awarded the previous year by the King of Denmark in person.

By local standards, Odaq was a wealthy man. The Explorers Club of New York had built his one-room hut, and gave him an income of $150 a year. The Danish Government gave him another $150 a year and arranged for an Eskimo woman to call on him every day to cook and clean up. Other villagers gave him food. He spent most of the time sitting beside the stove, snuffling and wheezing and coughing. While we were there, our guide tried to make conversation in Odaq's language. Odaq said little. Once or twice he pointed at a framed dim photograph of himself as a strong young hunter, nearly half a century ago, standing at the Pole with Peary.

Odaq's house was above average. Our guide led the way into another house closer to the shore. A man and his wife, two grown children, and three grandchildren lived here in two small rooms. The air was thick with fishy and ammoniacal odors. A partly skinned Arctic hare lay stiffly on a shelf. On one wall there were several reproductions of religious paintings.

The Eskimos were friendly. They offered limp brown hands for shaking, bared their empty gums in broad grins; and, in answer to all salutations, inquiries, and farewells, they kept nodding their heads and saying "Thank you, thank you, thank you."

When I got back to Baltimore nobody said "thank you." But about a month later Dorsey said: "There's some sort of Air Force junket to Alaska. You seem to be the Arctic expert, so you may as well go along."

12

Defense against possible Russian attack was again the theme. A score of American correspondents landed at Anchorage.

"If the Russians come across the Bering Strait, we'll bump them, and bump them hard," a general cheerfully assured us.

We watched six hundred Army paratroops tumble out of Flying Boxcars onto frozen tundra and silver birch trees near Big Delta, in central Alaska. Expert observers said it was a very successful drop; they were delighted that only seven men were injured; the casualty rate is often higher.

We were the guests of the Corps of Engineers and the local chamber of commerce at the Fairbanks Country Club, "The Farthest North Golf Club in the World." There I was trapped into making my first and last speech. I took as my subject the importance of the Mimeograph machine in the cold war. There was laughter, but I knew the speech wasn't really very good, and I vowed never to make another. Since then I have learned that invitations to make speeches are among the recurrent occupational hazards of journalism. Some reporters believe that the publicity does them good; they may be right. Some newspapers urge their men to accept all invitations from the papers' circulation areas. *The Sun* has never coerced its reporters to do so; and the average program chairman, however economy-minded, could be put off easily by the simple device of stuttering badly over the telephone or hinting broadly that one was subject to cataleptic seizures.

After the official tour of Alaska was over and the main party returned to Washington, I flew north to the Arctic Research Laboratory at Barrow, the territory's northernmost point.

The scientists at Barrow lived in rows of Quonset huts beside the Arctic Ocean. Under the auspices of the Johns Hopkins University and the Navy, they were working on all sorts of scientific projects whose applications, it was hoped, would help United States forces in cold countries. Some of the subjects being studied were "Fat Metabolism in Arctic Animals," "The Role of Lipids in the Adaptation of Animals to Cold," "The Blood Chemistry of Eskimos," "A Survey of Fishes of Northern Alaska," and "Respiratory Exchange in Man During Intensive Muscular Activity."

The directors of this research, important though the Pentagon said its military implications might be some day, sometimes tired of their work and looked for other things to do. Some of the scientists invited me to accompany them to an Eskimo dance, and, of course, I leaped at the opportunity.

"It won't be like a *nelakatuk*," I was warned by a man who was measuring the effects of permafrost on building foundations. A *nelaka-tuk*, he explained, is the all-night fiesta held each spring in celebration of the successes of the past whaling season. During a *nelakatuk* the Eskimos and their guests gorge themselves on *muk-tuk*, strips of raw whaleskin with thick chunks of blubber attached which taste like green walnuts and castor oil. Another favorite springtime delicacy, he said, is "Eskimo ice cream," walrus or whale blood and oil, beaten to a froth, frozen and served in lumps.

The Weasels' motors chugged explosively and their tracks crunched through crisp snow southwest along the coast toward the Eskimo village. We were wearing olive-green parkas with wolf fur around the hoods, and cumbersome "bunny boots," like divers' boots, made of canvas and white felt. The temperature was 35 degrees below freezing and it was falling. It was nearly 11 P.M.; there was no moon.

The village dance hall was a big Quonset hut. A group of young Eskimo men and women were shuffling about on the hard, squeaky snow. They were reluctant to go in. Eskimos are always very shy at the beginning of a dance.

Inside the bare hall the men and women were voluntary wallflowers, gathering around the edges of the room, whispering and softly giggling. The women were wearing loose, fur-trimmed long cotton dresses with flapper waistlines a little above the knees. All the dresses were of identical cut, but all the materials were different. The thick cottons were decorated with a wide variety of bright plaids, small-figured floral prints, and a few bolder designs that looked as though they had been intended for curtains in farm kitchens. The men's parkas were of solid colors of subdued tones. Men and women alike wore *muk-luks*, heavy fur boots of seal or caribou, ornately embroidered in bright colors.

As everyone was equally ungainly, ungainliness was quickly overlooked and new standards of beauty became evident. The Mongoloid faces were orange with red cheeks, flushed by the icy wind and the excitement of the occasion.

At 11:15, an hour after the dance was supposed to have begun, the floor was still empty. A row of naked electric bulbs hung from the curved ceiling and illuminated the splintery wooden boards.

Near an iron stove six musicians, men of late middle age, sat side by side in a row on the floor with their legs outstretched before them. Each man held in front of him a wooden hoop across which was fastened tightly-stretched skin from the liver of a whale, and a long, thin, flexible drumstick.

Without any sort of announcement or signal, the leader began beating the rim of his drum. The rhythm was steady and emphatic, closely approximating the rhythm of the normal human pulse. One by one, the other drummers followed the leader. Once the beat had been established in perfect unison, the leader began singing; and the others sang also. The song was simple and monotonous and had a powerful and stimulating effect. There were no words, only *aye-yaye-*

64

yayeing. The effect was this: it was as though six Moslems were chanting in imitation of Scottish bagpipes to the accompaniment of a chorus of restrained Dixieland drummers.

Each song (or section of the single, infinite song) began quietly, mounted rapidly in volume but not in tempo, and then abruptly came to a halt. Equally abruptly, after a brief pause, the music began again. Still there was no dancing.

The young women were gazing patiently at the dance floor. Several toothless old women were chewing in time with the music. At the far end of the hall, children, who were allowed to stay up all night on dance nights, wrestled and played tag.

The bandleader himself eventually got the dancing started. He put down his drum, stood facing the band, donned a pair of white cotton gloves, stamped his right foot, and gesticulated vigorously with his arms as though signaling in semaphore without the flags. It is a strict point of etiquette that an Eskimo man must put on gloves before dancing, though all the dancing is solo, without any contact with other dancers. The men always wear gloves. The women may carry theirs, but must show that they have them.

Following the leader's example, men and women of all ages, in twos and threes, left their places at the edge of the hall and took to the floor.

The dancing was strictly formalized. A dancer usually limited his entire performance to a spot a yard square, lifting a fur boot about eighteen inches from the floor and stamping it heavily in time with the drums while brandishing his gloved hands and slowly gyrating. Within this routine there was a considerable variety of mood and emphasis. Some of the women were graceful, almost languid; the men were more aggressive, more violent, more spasmodic, more exhibitionistic. The expressions on the women's faces suggested intense, introverted concentration, self-absorption. The men held their heads higher, jerked their jaws back and forth in stiff pecking motions, and grinned complacently. After each dance the dancers returned separately to their places, apparently quite unconcerned by any interest they might have aroused in each other.

"Do you ever dance with them?" I asked one of the scientists, the permafrost man.

"Good heavens, no!" he replied.

We left before 2 A.M. The dance was to continue all night. As we rode away, it occurred to me that reporters had something in common with scientists: we were all non-participating observers.

The next morning I attended a service in Barrow Presbyterian Church. It was half filled, mostly with women. Some of them had babies at their breasts. There were no young men. They had taken their rifles and skis after the dance and had flown away to practice defending the Arctic against the Russians.

13

The month after I got back from Alaska I was assigned to Korea. In January, 1953, the Korean War seemed to have reached a stalemate. The prospect of an indefinitely long separation from my family was not a pleasant one, but Susan and I agreed that the assignment represented professional progress; every newspaperman ought to be a war correspondent sooner or later.

On my way westward to the Far East I stopped in Hollywood for a couple of days, partly in order to give Jane Russell a copy of what I had written about her (I wanted her to know that I had tried), and partly for what I thought would be my final indulgence in the comforts of civilization before getting into battle dress and living like Hemingway during one of his more active periods.

I found Jane doing a song and dance number with Marilyn Monroe in a Paris café at Twentieth Century-Fox. They were finishing *Gentlemen Prefer Blondes*. While I was waiting to take Jane to lunch, I sat and talked with a studio press agent.

"Korea," he told me, when he learned where I was going, "is a real nothing now. Believe me; it's cold mashed potatoes." He thoughtfully cleaned his fingernails with a toothpick. "Nah," he said. "If I was you I'd tell them to shove it. What's the matter with those editors, putting you on a bum deal like that?"

"President Eisenhower has committed himself—" I began.

"I'm not saying *nobody* cares," the press agent conceded; "but for the public as a whole, it's nothing. Oh, sure, Keenan Wynn and a few of the other kids have been out there recently on personal appearance tours. But frankly they were wasting their time. Let's face it: Korea just ain't what it used to be; it's lost its impact. Why should anybody that is anybody waste their time going there any more?"

At Pearl Harbor, I was taken in the admiral's barge to see the almost totally submerged wreckage of the U.S.S. *Arizona*, one of the battleships put out of action by the Japanese air raid of December 7, 1941. The Chief of Staff of Pacific command headquarters, U.S. Navy, told me that the Pacific Fleet had already used more ammunition in the Korean War than the entire Navy used in all World War Two.

At Waikiki, under a giant banyan tree on the forecourt of the Moana Hotel, overlooking the beach and the breakers, I encountered Mr. and Mrs. Robert Hoyt, whom I had met in Fairbanks, Alaska.

"We've taken a house on the beach for a month," Mrs. Hoyt said. "Why don't you come and stay with us instead of in a hotel?"

"Thanks, but I have to go to Korea," I said.

Mr. Hoyt became busy ordering more daiquiris. After a while, he turned to me and said: "Have you ever ridden one of these surfboards? I've been riding one all day. Is it rugged! I had a boy push me ahead of the right waves—but it's the paddling out again that gets you. Tomorrow I'm going to hire another boy to push me out. You know what? There ought to be a surfboard-tow, like a ski-lift. I wonder why nobody ever tried that? I bet somebody could clean up."

I was anti-Japanese and pious about the Korean War until I got to Japan and Korea.

In Tokyo I checked into the Press Club, in Shimbun Alley. I was sitting in the lounge drinking gimlets, with nothing to do but wait for the Far East Command, U.S. Army, to issue me my military uniforms and a Noncombatant's Certificate of Identity (I was going to have my war and avoid it too), when I met Patrick O'Donovan, of the London *Observer*. He was a striking figure, a tall man with long, disorderly, dark Irish hair, a luxuriantly livid face, a dark-gray flannel suit with Edwardian cuffs and narrow legs, a loosely knotted tie of pale-peach silk, a small yellow boutonnière, cream socks, and sand-colored suède shoes. I asked him what he was doing in Japan while waiting to go to Korea.

"Really!" he protested. "I'm not *waiting* in Japan. I'm entering a Zen Buddhist monastery. I shall write a most important article."

"Aren't you going to Korea?" I asked. At the moment, I could think of nothing else.

"All in good time," he said. "There's some jade in Kyoto that I must see. And they haven't finished renovating my Korean screen. You haven't been to Korea yet, I gather?" I admitted that I hadn't.

"Well, there's nothing going on there, so I wouldn't hurry, if I were you." He asked me where I was staying. When I said the Press Club he looked aghast.

"You *can't*," he said. "It's *ghastly*. Photographers and Australians and their *squalid* friends. The midnight crash of furniture through windows. The most *adolescent* sexual boasting. No, not the Press Club."

A young Japanese with serious glasses, neatly combed black hair, and the respectable attire of a Western bank clerk came up to O'Donovan's chair and inclined his head in salutation.

"Ah, Juzo!" O'Donovan said. "This is Juzo Fukunaka. Mr. Catlingsan. Juzo: you're late."

"Yes, Mr. O'Donovan. I had difficulty obtaining the Kabuki tickets."

"That is no excuse."

"The *yukatas* and fans, Mr. O'Donovan. They had not been packed before my arrival at the shop."

"You should have instructed them better. It's just not good enough, Juzo. You really are a very naughty interpreter."

69

"Yes, Mr. O'Donovan. I am sorry."

"Well, at least be sure to call up and order dinner. Remember: master wants thrush."

"Yes, thrush."

O'Donovan, I learned later, had traveled extensively in Africa. Being in fact liberal and humane, he enjoyed assuming the scolding manner of a severe district commissioner addressing one of his lazier, stupider houseboys. Juzo, a graduate of Waseda University, didn't really get the joke; but he seemed to know that there was one, for his smile did not appear to be a smile of Oriental embarrassment.

"Do you like thrush?" O'Donovan asked me. "Perhaps you would like to join me for dinner. I am staying in a Japanese hotel. There are no other Europeans in it. If you like it, you may move there. I'm sure it would be better for you than this place.

"Juzo is an excellent interpreter," O'Donovan went on. "He did terribly well at university. Waseda is certainly the most distinguished university in Tokyo. You have got an interpreter, I suppose? No? No wonder you haven't ventured out of the Press Club. You must have an interpreter. Some correspondents stay here for months and never go anywhere but the Foreign Office and Tachikawa Airport. I know what: you can share Juzo if you pay half his salary."

"Here we are," O'Donovan said, as the small Japanese taxi slithered to a halt. "It's not a bad place, really."

The driver gave profuse, sibilant thanks for the 120 yen (35 cents). The taxi rattled away. We were left in darkness, on a deserted street between a faintly gleaming canal and a large building with wings extending to the sidewalk and embracing an obscure little garden. As we walked along the stone pathway to the building's unadorned front entrance, O'Donovan said, in the confidential manner one might adopt when warning a friend about the quirks of one's mad relations: "Don't walk on their woodwork with your shoes on. They get most frightfully offended if you do. They're easily offended."

The foyer bore no resemblance to the foyer of an American hotel. There were no uniformed porters and bellboys, no marble and plush, no illuminated signs pointing the ways to barbershop and bar, no newsstand, no registration desk, no elevators. We were in a

70

bare room of polished dark wood. There were two wooden receptacles for umbrellas, a wall of open pigeonholes for shoes, and a cupboard for coats. And that was all. O'Donovan removed his shoes and thrust his feet into flat, open, leather slippers. In order to keep the slippers from falling off one had to shuffle; the Japanese gait came naturally. We walked up bare wooden stairs to the second floor. O'Donovan opened a sliding door made of paperboard in a light wooden frame. His suite was in three parts: an antechamber, a square room measuring about fifteen feet each way, and a small balcony looking out on stunted trees and shrubs. The partition between the room and the balcony consisted of delicate wooden windows with translucent white paper panes. The windows, the antechamber partitions, and the hall doors could all slide in sections in a variety of combinations, giving the impression of a magician's cabinet.

The furnishings were simple and few, built close to the fine, rice-straw mats that completely covered and partly insulated the cold floor. The dressing table was no more than a foot above the matting. The narrow mirror, about a yard tall, was modestly concealed in an embroidered cotton bag. The telephone table was nine inches high. The square dining table, made of a dark wood that looked like walnut, was eighteen inches high. Fat pillows had been arranged around the table on two sides. There were two hard-upholstered elbow rests.

The decorations were water colors of a scowling Chinese devil, and two squirrels on a bough. There was a miniature flowering shrub in a ceramic bowl in the prayer niche. Heat was provided by glowing charcoal on a bed of sand in a heavy, squat, carved wooden bowl with a copper lining.

Two Japanese serving girls twittered prettily outside the door. O'Donovan summoned them in. They genuflected and prostrated themselves in the doorway, crossed the room with bowed heads, and crawled around the table with our hors d'oeuvres. Their attitudes and gestures of humility were so formal and graceful that they achieved a peculiar dignity.

Celery, asparagus, young cucumber, and pickles were succeeded by almost colorless, almost tasteless consommé, and this in turn was succeeded by golden-brown, plump, soft little birds, which had been decapitated and dressed in the ordinary way, except that they still had their tiny claws, now curled up together in a pitiable supplicatory gesture.

"The feet are delicious," O'Donovan said. They were as delicately crisp as the extremities of fried soft crabs.

Halfway through this dainty meal there was a crescendo of uneven thuds in the hall. A maid scuttled into the room, perfunctorily touched her forehead to the matting, and urgently babbled what we guessed correctly was a warning that there was an unmanageable intruder. There was a snarl of rage outside and a torrent of Chaucerian epithets.

"It's all right," O'Donovan resignedly told the maid. "My friend." She looked uncomprehending. O'Donovan pointed to the doors and to himself. "Friendo," he explained.

"Friendo!" the maid exclaimed, relieved. "Ah-so!" She quickly slid open a door and a British Army captain, who looked grotesquely clumsy beside her—he was in fact grotesquely clumsy—lurched into the room. He had the face of an albino rabbit with an unsuitably heavy, straw-colored moustache and glazed pale eyes.

"On leave," he said.

"Do come in," O'Donovan said with wasted sarcasm. "There will be a third for dinner," he informed the maid. "Chop for this bwana. Food. My," he said to the captain, "you *are* drunk. I have never been able to understand why the Eighth Army speaks of 'Rest and Recreation'; quite obviously, one can't have both on a short leave from Korea. Buzz: you've got your shoes on."

The captain took his shoes off; they fell off his long khaki feet in different directions. He sat heavily on a cushion beside the table and began tearing with his hands one of the remaining thrushes.

"The Japanese are extraordinarily kind to people who are drunk," O'Donovan said. "They are considered to be in a condition of special privilege, requiring special care."

Later, we changed into kimonos and shuffled down the hall to a tiled room where an outsize wooden bathtub was set into the floor. A wall panel slid open and the custodian of the bathroom climbed through with towels and soap. The cleaning was done outside the

72

bath. The Japanese scrubbed our backs while we sat on miniature stools and poured innumerable wooden buckets of hot water over us. Then we descended into the tub. The water was nearly chest-deep, faintly redolent of sandalwood and almost boiling. A lobster's death perhaps is not the worst: after the first shock, I felt pleasantly faint and disembodied, quite weightless, and devoid of thoughts. . . .

During our absence, maids had arranged sleeping bags made of soft, thick eiderdown quilts, on the floor. They contained large glazed-earthenware hot-water bottles. I experienced the most delightful lassitude, an awareness of a softening of the bones of the spine and the toes, as I lay back, acquiescently listening to the captain and, surprisingly, O'Donovan, singing "Rule, Britannia!" out of tune, very loud.

It was morning. The windows were partly open. Birdsong. A distant cacophony of automobile horns. The foliage of an evergreen was silhouetted against white sky. There was a faint aroma of hot tea beside my pillow. I had slept well.

"What's this place?" asked an unenthusiastic voice.

"Oh, shut up, Buzz," another voice replied.

"Fukunaka-san comes," said a maid.

"Mr. O'Donovan: I have brought you the newspapers," Juzo said.

"Oh, Christ!" Donovan complained, burrowing deeper under his quilt. "Nag, nag, nag. . . . Is there no end to it?"

Juzo had some tea and translated some of the Tokyo headlines and editorial articles for me. He was especially interested himself in an account of the annual poetry recital at the Imperial Palace. Royal poetry readings were instituted in 1483, he said. Each year thousands of Japanese submitted poems composed on a theme announced by the Palace. The theme for 1953 was "Outgoing Ship." I wrote down some of them.

The next day, I gathered my identity cards (correspondents were given the simulated rank of "major through colonel," for the sake of prison-camp conventions; at liberty they retained civilian immunity to the formalities of the military hierarchy), my "invitational travel orders" (tickets for an unlimited number of free flights in U.S. Air Force planes between Japan and Korea), a duffle bag full of khaki clothing, and my Olivetti portable and cameras.

I took a taxi to Tachikawa and committed myself to the most dreadful plane of all, a double-decker transport like a tin whale, a Globemaster, bound for Seoul. There were 110 other passengers, all soldiers. As I sat strapped to a canvas bench I read the Japanese Crown Prince's poem for 1953:

> "Across the surging seas
> To new and wondrous worlds I sail."

14

"Operation Smack," a Seventh Division raid against Chinese positions on the western front of Korea, began the night I arrived in Seoul. That night the Air Force dropped a lot of bombs to soften the defenses. More air raids and artillery fire continued the attack the following morning. At one o'clock in the afternoon tanks and infantry advanced. The operation was the largest so far that year, but in most respects it was like many others during that period of curiously old-fashioned warfare.

The objects of the operation were to destroy Chinese bunkers, kill Chinese soldiers, take Chinese prisoners, search for weaknesses in the Chinese line, prevent the Chinese from burrowing closer to U.N. territory, improve U.N. battle techniques, and return to base. The infantry action began punctually and lasted four and a half hours. The Seventh Division failed to reach the top of "Spud Hill," its main objective. Accurate and intense Chinese machine-gun fire, mortar fire, and grenades drove the Americans back. No Chinese prisoners were taken. Three Americans were killed and sixty-one were wounded.

In the Seoul press billets the night after the operation, an Associated Press reporter showed me a document that struck me, a newcomer to Korea, as extraordinary. It was a detailed battle scenario, or timetable, bound in a handsome cover stamped "Secret: Security Information—Operation Smack," and imprinted with the insignia of the Seventh Division in red, blue, and black. Correspondents who had been covering the Korean War on and off since it had begun said that they had never before seen anything quite like this; the scenario was unprecedentedly elaborate. It had been distributed before the raid to numerous U.N. correspondents and Air Force and Army observers who had been invited as witnesses. The program notes explained that the raid (which had been conceived weeks before) was supposed to show "the manner in which the infantry can take maximum advantage of shock action. . . ." Special observation bunkers, heated with stoves, were provided for the guests, who were instructed to remain under cover "during the entire operation."

Even as a newcomer, I thought it obvious that the raid had been a bad flop as a "shock action," and I couldn't help wondering whether it was only a coincidence that the failure had been preceded by such extraordinary ballyhoo.

In the cable to my paper, I called the element of showmanship "a strange innovation." I wrote nothing to suggest that there might have been a security leak, though I believed then, and I still believe, that there might have been. I simply described the preparations for the raid, the arrangements for spectators, the raid itself as reported by the Army, and the raid's lamentable results.

There was a political explosion in the United States. A congressional inquiry was demanded. The Chicago *Tribune* called the raid "a specimen slaughter." The New York *Daily News* blamed it on "a criminal lapse of judgment." An editorial in the Baltimore *Sun* said that "Operation Smack" left "a decidedly bad taste in the mouth." Representative Clare E. Hoffman (R., Mich.) recalled gladiators who died for the amusement of Roman emperors. William G. Bray (R., Ind.) was as "mad as hell."

I found myself with some unwelcome allies. I had been ardently in agreement with President Truman's decision to intervene in Korea; but now people began criticizing the raid in the ways in which they had criticized U.N. intervention; people against the intervention seemed to deplore "Operation Smack" automatically; the immediate issues became muddled.

The end of the unpleasantness was hastened by General J. Lawton Collins, Army Chief of Staff, in Washington. General Collins pointed out reproachfully that the whole controversy had been caused by the report of "a single man," but added: "I offer no brief whatsoever for the eager beaver [the Seventh Division public information officer who assembled the operational plans under a cover bearing the division insignia]. That was a mistake. The Army accepts it as a mistake and regrets it."

15

Seoul was a gray city, especially on the cold winter days when I first explored it. Most of the Koreans who lived there were ill housed, ill heated, ill clad, and ill fed. Twice the war had raked up and down the peninsula, ruining parts of Seoul in passing; yet the United Nations, each time it regained control of the city, discovered that the population had increased. Families from the villages had come to the city for security, though the dangers had sometimes proved far greater there than in the rice paddies. Many of the refugees stayed. Now, with the military front stabilized thirty miles to the north and approximately half the buildings of Seoul destroyed or damaged, the civilian population of the city was believed to exceed a million. But the squalor of overcrowding was never as obvious in Seoul as in Pusan, the southeastern port, where men, women, and children slept in rows on downtown sidewalks at night like corpses arranged neatly after a disaster. In Seoul the human congestion was mostly hidden in honeycombs of domestic architecture: closely grouped gray houses built around patios. Attached to these were ugly growths of improvised shelters: shacks, coops and kennels made of packing-case lumber, corrugated cardboard, flattened beer cans, and any other materials that could be salvaged from Army waste or filched from Army depots and adapted to construction.

But the basic framework of the city, the inner grid of boulevards, the cardinal gateways, the temples and royal palaces and walled gardens, had endured everything in bleak grandeur. Seoul was a place of broad vistas extended by destruction. There were new empty spaces. Between the large Japanese-built municipal buildings there were gaps, heaps of concrete rubble and twisted metal. Behind many grand façades there was only sky. Everywhere one smelled the cold, cement smell of modern catastrophe.

The pale winter sunlight slowly dissipated the smoky haze over the city. Korean military policewomen wearing khaki uniforms stood on wooden podia at the intersections of main roads and directed weapons carriers and Army trucks. Children in khaki rags carried loads of firewood on A-frames on their backs, or tried to sell worthless goods to soldiers. Old Korean men in long white robes and Western hats ambled purposelessly, or sat on benches and waited. The domed Capitol, a gray shell, black inside, symbolized the state of South Korean politics.

In all that miserable city there were only a few men who were altogether free and reasonably content with what they were doing. They were the correspondents who lived in the United Nations press billets, a flat-roofed Japanese apartment house in a compound enclosed by a barbed-wire fence. In this place there was institutional security for which the inmates were not responsible; there were privileges without duties; there were interesting things to learn, whenever one felt like learning them; there was plenty of food and drink and service. Living there was like living in a pleasantly eccentric progressive boarding school, with unlimited pocket money, and without any teachers and rules. It was fascinating to observe how different individuals behaved in these circumstances; and the fascination was not spoiled even by the fact that childish quarreling sometimes broke out over trivialities.

If personalities, cliques, and coalitions began to grate on one's nerves, one could always go away and observe the war for a while.

Newspapermen were most heartily welcomed and treated as grown-ups, even if not invariably cordially liked, by the numerous rival military units that made up the complicated patchwork of the United Nations Command; transportation by land, sea, and air and guided tours and explanations were available for the asking.

The man who had achieved the most harmonious adjustment to the life of the press billets was the senior continuous resident, John Ridley, of the London *Daily Telegraph*. While some other correspondents, merely pausing in transit, lived in casual disorder in rooms whose only furniture was a GI camp bed, a rickety desk, and a straight-backed wooden chair, Ridley presided over an establishment that was a marvel of acquisition, efficiency, and sentiment. He had two rooms, one for his Korean houseboy, a vain, petulant young man of whom Ridley was strangely fond. The larger room was Ridley's bedroom, drawing room, office, library, menagerie, and bar. It was arranged as carefully as a captain's cabin. His beds were remarkably like the American hospital beds that had somehow found their way onto the Korean black market. His desk was as substantial as a bank manager's. He had carpets, chairs with cushions, and vases of flowers. There was a cupboard crowded with bottles of all sorts of liquors, wines, and beers. He maintained files of newspapers and official announcements. He had a shortwave radio. He kept a cat which he said he had found starving in the mountains near Seoul and had nursed to health; its name was Yao of the Imjin. The Imjin River was one of the U.N.'s principal natural defense lines north of Seoul. The cat was addressed as Yao, which is pronounced like the usual noise made by cats of all nationalities late at night. Its diet consisted of beef stew from the mess; its purr sounded like a dog's growl; it switched its tail from side to side when gratified, and its favorite sport was retrieving a ball made of Army press releases.

In addition to the houseboy and Yao, Ridley's pets included a parrot and a goldfish. Because of his concern for their comfort it was only after lengthy discussion and careful planning that Ridley felt he could leave the building. Unless something very special was happening at Commonwealth Division H.Q., he usually restricted his movements to the weekly drive with his houseboy to the Seoul NAAFI, an admirable British institution, something like a post exchange, but with the important addition of a well stocked, tax-free liquor store.

Ridley was a man of about forty years of age and of unimposing stature; his face, however, was already impressively rubicund, and he had a wonderfully rich voice, strained through clenched teeth, and a country gentlemanly laugh. He never recited his personal history, but much of it could be easily constructed from his remarks. For instance, he would look somberly into his gin and bitters and say: "It's a terrible thing to have to cut a man's throat while he's asleep [long pause]. But [sigh] one had one's duty to perform. That was the sort of thing one simply had to do if one wanted to serve with the Maquis in Occupied France."

The story I eventually pieced together, with his help, was this: Ridley was the scion of a distinguished aristocratic family that had (or had had) vast estates in Northumberland. He went to Spain during the Civil War (as a playboy, to learn to fight bulls, to volunteer for one army or another) and married a young Spanish lady of flawless beauty. She gave birth to a son and was killed immediately afterward by aerial bombing. The boy was entrusted to Ridley's grandparents and Ridley vowed to spend the rest of his life as an exile. He had been fighting in wars, or covering them as a correspondent, ever since. He had acquired a house in Paris and would retire, some day, to the Riviera.

I still don't know for certain all the actualities of his life. Sometimes, to avoid monotony, he varied the details. But he could be a charming host in his room in the Seoul press billets. He had a highly developed social sense which he applied seriously to the social chaos of that remote place. He delighted in sending notes by his houseboy inviting other correspondents in the building to his room for sherry and biscuits at 11 A.M. Some people laughed at this ritual; but nobody who was invited failed to attend. On these occasions, as on others, Ridley wore a Paisley silk scarf inside the open collar of his stiffly pressed British tropical khakis. His shoes gleamed like old mahogany. He would receive his guests punctiliously, ushering them to their places, inquiring after their health, and relaying their orders for drinks to the houseboy. The gracious effect was only partly marred by the fact that the small dimensions of the room and the number of guests ordinarily resulted in some of us sitting on beds, knee to knee, while others squeezed by and the houseboy was squashed against the open cupboard that served as the bar.

At times, as the canapés were handed around, Ridley's conversational mannerisms suggested *The Tatler* or *The Field*. He referred to President Rhee as though he were the lord lieutenant of the county, and to the people of South Korea as though they were devoted but troublesome tenants whose manifestations of discontent with the United Nations (the Ministry of Agriculture & Fisheries) caused him affectionate anxiety even as it won his secret sympathy.

The hospitality Ridley offered and his genuine interest in the people who accepted it brought him a great deal of information about what was going on in the war, and he was such an experienced journalist that he was able, by putting together facts from many sources, to produce articles that were often more complete and every bit as vivid as those written by some of the correspondents who had done a great deal of tiring legwork to get them.

"My task," he would say, as he refreshed an exhausted reporter just back from some minor action at the front, "is to stay close to the center of things. I had a *very* interesting little talk this morning with a colonel from K-Com-Z. If you'll keep this to yourself, I feel that it would be quite in order for me to tell you some of the things he said. They help put so many of the tactical details into perspective. But tell me about *your* day. Are you absolutely exhausted? Where have you been? Whom did you lunch with? What's happening?"

Ridley was a brain-picker par excellence. But his main achievement, he used to say, was to demonstrate that one could be a foreign correspondent and still be a gentleman.

16

In the first week of February, 1953, a few days after President Eisenhower had ostentatiously ordered the U.S. Seventh Fleet out of the Formosa Strait and so had removed the immediate obstacle between the armed forces of Nationalist China and China proper, I took the opportunity to do some Far Eastern sightseeing. The pretext was sound: some Western commentators were saying with straight faces that Chiang Kai-shek would now be able to "unleash" his troops; the Nationalists were free to invade the Chinese mainland, and so to reduce China's capacity to wage war in Korea.

I was in such a hurry that instead of returning first to Tokyo, where I could have obtained a Nationalist Chinese visa, I flew by Chinese Air Transport (the late General C. L. Chennault's airline), from Pusan, Korea, direct to Taipei, the capital of Formosa. I counted on being able to talk my way from the airport to the Nationalist foreign ministry, where I would have been able, probably, to get permission to stay on the island for a few weeks. But the airport officials were adamant in their refusal to let me enter the country in this unorthodox fashion. I was ordered back into the plane, which was bound for Hong Kong. Professionally, I was thwarted; personally, I could hardly have been better pleased.

Hong Kong makes one feel like a millionaire. It does this by measuring one with a tape measure late in the afternoon and delivering an excellent suit to one's hotel room by breakfast time the next morning. I also got a tailor-made waistcoat in Burgundy-red brocade decorated with Pegasuses of many colors, an invaluable good-luck charm for use at race tracks and during air travel.

Because Britain recognized the government in Peiping, there was no Nationalist Chinese diplomatic representative in Hong Kong; I had to arrange to go to the nearest place where there was one. This place was Macao, a Portuguese colony farther west on the South China coast and about four hours away by steamer.

My cable from Korea suggesting that I should visit Formosa had not been worded interrogatively. It had said something like this: "UNLESS YOU IMMEDIATELY INSTRUCT CONTRARIWISE AM LEAVING NEXT AVAILABLE PLANE TAIPEIWARDS INVESTIGATE EFFECTS WITHDRAWAL SEVENTH FLEET." I had waited for an answer as long as it takes to pack a toothbrush. As I still didn't really know how enthusiastic my office was about my suggestion, I became a trifle uneasy as I waited for a Portuguese visa to prolong my journey in the wrong direction.

To soothe my nerves, I sought distraction in the Tiger Balm Gardens, a colossal, gorgeously vulgar, many-terraced hillside shrine that had been constructed by Aw Boon Haw, a Chinese multimillionaire, in honor of himself and Tiger Balm, the aromatic pink ointment panacea that had made his fortune. The spirits of Hieronymus Bosch, Barnum and Bailey, and George Washington Hill were embodied in hundreds of weirdly imaginative, garishly painted concrete statues, tableaux, and frescoes in bas relief.

Between flower bushes were pits containing stone anteaters, boars, serpents, gorgons, hippogriffs, dragons, and dodos, misshapen accidents of evolution and myth that looked as though they could never have happened, but that were, at the same time, dimly recognizable, familiar enemies from the dark corners of the mind.

Chinese parents slowly conducted their children past frescoes depicting dead wicked Chinese in their traditional hell. The frescoes showed in ghastly detail many sorts of punitive butchery, and torture by fire and water. The punishments fitted the crimes: a man who had been a gossip on earth was having his tongue torn out; a mortal glutton was suffering eternal disembowelment; sexual libertines were having an awful time.

The gardens had their less terrifying aspects. There was a mermaid with slanting Oriental eyes. A Chinese amateur photographer posed his small boy in a litter of concrete sucklings that were nuzzling at a giant black concrete sow, while the boy's mother giggled with a hand politely covering her mouth.

Being a place of harmless nightmares, the gardens were very popular with children, who ran along the intricate maze of narrow paths, between beetling artificial cliffs, across small humpbacked bridges, up steep, twisting stairways, and, at every turn where they were confronted with grotesque monsters, yelped and squealed with the special tremulous fearful delight that one experiences when encountering apparent dangers that are known to be not really dangerous at all.

I thought that another multimillionaire should acquire a remote island and build there a Garden of Warfare, in which all the world's generals and most of its politicians would be permanently confined, to run compulsorily along harmless trenches, to discover awful new secret weapons, all made of painted concrete.

There was just enough time to catch the motor vessel *Lee Hong* for Macao. When one is rushing to catch transportation, even on a holiday, the journey suddenly seems vital, so I forgot that *The Sun* might not approve of my methods. (I later learned that [a] my methods were not uniquely mine and [b] editors usually don't care how one gets to a story, as long as one gets there.)

In the saloon of the *Lee Hong* I met Michael Patrick O'Brien, alias Robert Stephens, alias Stephen Stanley Ragan, a stateless vagrant who had got aboard at Macao more than three hundred trips before. Now neither Hong Kong nor Macao would let him go ashore again.

He told me a lurid story of reformatories, jails, and military stockades, of holdups in the United States and some trouble with a knife in a Shanghai night club. It was a great story. I envisioned the late Humphrey Bogart in the part. O'Brien and I shared half a bottle of "No. 1 Scotch Whiskey: Guaranteed First Class Edinburgh Grapes." I wrote a letter, which he signed, asking Mrs. Eleanor Roosevelt to persuade some country to take him. She had been engaged in the composition of the United Nations bill of human rights, and it seemed to O'Brien and me that one basic human right ought to be the right to get off the *Lee Hong*. But O'Brien was not an ideal candidate for citizenship anywhere, as he himself conceded.

Many months later I read somewhere that he had been accepted by the Dominican Republic. I don't know how he got there. But I imagine that O'Brien and President Trujillo understand each other and get along together just fine. They deserve each other.

17

When engaged in conversational off-the-beaten-trackmanship, I find there's no place in the world more certain to score points than Macao. Whitehorse has the pleasant, old-fashioned simplicity about it of Yukon River paddle boats; Tegucigalpa has a sprightly nursery-rhyme rhythm; Reykjavik suggests austere cragginess and the darkness of Icelandic sagas; Maiduguri, with its repeated long *u*, phonetically calls to mind the mystery of ju-ju; but for all-around exoticism, combining Latin and Oriental allures, hot blood and secret eyes, there's nothing to excel Macao. One of the compensatory joys of the foreign correspondent, on his visits to friends prospering as investment brokers and insurance salesmen, is to be able to sit back over the afterdinner brandy and to reminisce. How satisfying it is, when a moss-gathering worker-friend recalls the quaint little sea-food restaurant he discovered last summer in Massachusetts, to be able to say: "Ah, yes; sea food! Curiously enough, the best octopus I ever tasted was prepared by the chef at the Bella Vista in Macao;

a most attractive hotel—running down a bit by now though, I fear. Wasn't it Sir John Bowring who wrote that charming little poem that begins, 'Gem of the Orient earth and open sea, Macao! . . .'? How nice it was in the evenings, sitting on the terrace, high on the hillside, looking at the junks, with sails like bats' wings, and the hills of Taipa, darkening between the pink and silver water and the pink and gray sky. . . ."

That much is only the thin end of the wedge, and it is already futile for other conversationalists to nominate the charms of Paris and Rome. Macao is stronger stuff. Hardly anybody has been there. Who, ordinarily, would go there, except young or unsuccessful diplomats, espionage agents, smugglers of bullion and opium, arms racketeers, gamblers and whores and fugitives, dealers in pornography, and newspapermen in need of Nationalist Chinese visas? And yet, in its special ways, Macao is as glamorous in its infamy as French Guiana—and Macao, of course, has a better climate.

There is as much commercial opportunism and intrigue in Hong Kong. But Hong Kong has a British air of legality and public virtue: Hong Kong has massive banks, London buses, the Royal Navy, British officers' wives with prohibitively wholesome faces, even a cricket ground where tea is served in the pavilion. Generations of strict colonial training have produced Chinese policemen who look fairly honest and, if they don't look absolutely honest, they at least have shiny buttons.

Macao is decadent and dirty, cruel and corrupt. The natives of Macao converted the missionaries. Macao is practically an island; it feels like one. In fact, it is a peninsula, about three miles long and a mile across at the widest part, connected with the coast of Kwangtung Province by an isthmus only a few hundred yards wide.

The short international frontier is marked by a high, ornamental arch called the Barrier Gate. It is guarded by Communist Chinese soldiers on the north side and by Portuguese African soldiers on the south. The Africans are from Mozambique; they're large and tough and sensitive about being black. A few months before my visit some Chinese sentries teased the Africans on duty about the color of their skin. The Africans retorted first with rifles, then with machine guns, then with mortars. The exchange of fire was so fierce, and the casualties so numerous, mostly Chinese, that Dr. P. J. Lobo, himself, personally intervened, negotiated with the local Communist commander, and, it was said, personally paid him several tens of thousands of dollars in reparations in order to restore order. The incident and the quiet, businesslike way it was settled were typical of Macao; there was no ugly publicity, no recourse to the International Court of Justice or the United Nations, or, indeed, to diplomatic channels at all. The diplomats stationed in Macao were busy enough, during their brief office hours, turning down applicants for passports and visas. International crises, like most other matters of major importance to Macao, were handled with authoritative dispatch by Dr. Lobo.

Dr. Lobo was a Eurasian whose official title was Director of Economic Services. Unofficially he was known as "Mr. Macao." A large part of the wealth on which his power was based had been accumulated, and was still being accumulated, by importing gold from the West and selling it to the highest bidders in the East. In 1953 he was said to have a private Catalina flying boat that brought a load of ingots into Macao once a week. To import gold, one had to have a government license; only Dr. Lobo could get the licenses. About 190,000 of the 200,000 people of Macao were Chinese; the principal food was rice. Dr. Lobo and his associates were said to monopolize the rice business and to keep the price profitably high. Dr. Lobo's name was invoked or sadly referred to in almost every conversation about the affairs of Macao. When minor government officials did not mention his name one could read it in their nervous eyes. But Dr. Lobo, like Nero and Al Capone, had his tender moments of cultural divertissement. He wrote sentimental semiclassical music, conducted his own orchestral recordings of it, and broadcast the records over his own radio station.

Macao is hilly, rising steeply from the cluttered wharves to several round peaks, sites of the Old Fortress of Mong Ha, the Guia Lighthouse, Old Monte Fortress, the Cathedral, and the Bishop's Palace. Around the edges and in the European sections, Macao at first looked like a run-down city in northern Brazil. The buildings of Macao have the same terra cotta tiles and flat façades of stucco, washed in pastel pinks and yellows and blues and greens, cracking and crumbling like the icing of stale cakes. There were some wide avenues shaded by wide-spreading trees. Some of the statelier houses were embellished with fine, intricate wrought-iron gates and balcony railings and with blue-and-white religious tiles set into outside walls. The cemetery dates from the sixteenth century, when the colony was founded. The names on the graves are Portuguese. A bronze bust of Vasco da Gama and a heroic equestrian statue on the Avenida Dr. Oliveira Salazar proclaimed continuing Portuguese sovereignty; but one rarely forgot that one was really in China, and that Macao's separate existence depended on its usefulness to the Communist régime. Macao has always been mainly an entrepot, a tax-free port through which East-West trade could be transacted profitably. Even the Government Propaganda Section, a sleepy office that nobody seemed to take seriously, was unable to produce an impressive list of Macao's own resources. The major products were fish, matches, firecrackers, incense sticks, cloth goods, preserves, vegetable oils, Chinese wines and cigarettes, worth a total of about $17,000,000 a year. At the same time brokers dealt in transshipments worth about $150,000,000.

During my short stay O'Brien, the man on the *Lee Hong*, began to seem quite normal compared with some of the individuals who solicited my help. While contraband strategic materials were pouring through Macao from Western factories to China and the Communist armies in North Korea, many people who lacked travel documents and the means to buy them were stuck in the colony. One Japanese tried to win my sympathy by saying that he was a newspaperman himself; he had been a prisoner of war in China; he had escaped and missed repatriation; and he was longing to get back to his sister, who he claimed was none other than "Tokyo Rose." An Armenian and his wife offered to allow me to invest twelve hundred American dollars in an Arabian oil company; he needed the money to sail to Bahrein to claim his share of the profits; I would be richly rewarded.

I met three RAF officers in mufti, a medical officer and two pilots, who had come over to Macao from Hong Kong for the weekend. They were drinking in the hotel bar.

"We're going to do the town tonight," one of them said. "Do you want to join us?" I felt then, as always, that the wider the scope of my knowledge of the world, the more valuable I could be to my paper. It was my duty to go along.

We were in a casino.

"You like playing the games?" asked a woman who must have been at least sixty years of age. She looked like a warning in a Hogarth engraving. She had soot-black hair, a chalk-white complexion, false eyelashes like spiders, a scarlet mouth, and gold and black teeth. Her fat arms were blue-white and as flaccid and wrinkled as balloons long after a party. Her corset was so tight that excess flesh, squeezed upward, bulged into her armpits.

"I am Russian lady," the woman said. "White Russian."

"A countess in distress," it was suggested.

"You are clever man," she said. "You have heard of me? Yes, I am countess. But all that," she added tragically, "has gone. I have been in China many years."

"Many, many," said the medical officer.

"Which man will marry me and take me to England?" she asked brightly, chuckling when we recoiled. I wondered how long she had been making jokes about her own startling ugliness. "What's a matter?" she scolded, "you no like jig-a-jig?"

"We like jig-a-jig, yes," somebody said.

"You like to see?" she asked. "I show films. I show South Sea island film—very pretty man, pretty girl, make jig-a-jig on the beach, best you ever saw. Also Paris film—two girls, one man, very naughty, do everything."

The synopses were not altogether unappealing.

"Do you think we'll have our throats cut?" I asked.

"You're safer walking the back streets of Macao than the streets of Soho," one of my companions said.

"I've heard that the local authorities are very strict about the murder of Europeans," the doctor said. "Informers are well rewarded; there's no way of escaping from the colony; culprits are punished with exemplary speed and severity."

"Then what are we waiting for?"

"What indeed?"

The old hag led the way between the vertical signboards of Chinese stores, along cobbled alleyways foul with sewage and the garlic steam from cooking pots, through a doorway, up a flight of stairs, through a beaded string curtain and into a dingy dining room. We sat on chairs that were lumpy with broken springs. A boy brought Chinese beer at five times the usual price. A Chinese man in a shabby suit looked up to appraise us, then went on threading film through a projector aimed at a sheet on the wall. The lights went out. There was a loud whirring and a flickering beam of dusty yellow light cast forth the images of two women undressing a man in the frenetic, jerky manner of Keystone cops. The scene was a Western living room furnished in Department Store Modern, c. 1925, the year I was born.

"It's very sexy," the Russian woman assured us apprehensively. Our conversation was not serious.

"I think you like the South Sea island better," she said, secreting our money in her crepe bosom. "You wait and see: it's more pretty people. This is more naughty; but that is more pretty."

"But this one's very funny," I gallantly conceded. The man was wearing a wristwatch and socks held up with elastic suspenders. His lugubrious long face reminded me of a certain *Sun* political reporter. He wasn't much of an actor—he looked now as though he were suffering an acute attack of heartburn; the grimace evidently represented passion; even so, he was acting a lot better than he wrote politics, I thought.

"You can buy a copy of this film," the hostess said, as the three twitching contortionists on the wall achieved their ultimate entanglement. "You take it home, you never have to work again."

"Reminds me rather of rugger, this bit," one of the pilots said. "A scrum, you know."

"One hundred pounds sterling," she said.

"Shut up about money and show us the second one," the other pilot suggested.

The second film was a bit highbrow in the beginning: there were palm trees and surf. A rather plump Polynesian fisherman, or perhaps a Hawaiian cook, or just possibly a Turkish weightlifter, and a girl with long hair with a flower in it, stood face to face, holding hands, smiling.

"Hey, what's this?" one of us demanded.

"It's O.K.," our hostess promised. "You wait and see. Very nice film, very dirty, everyone like it."

After the initial romantic suspense, the director had concentrated on extreme close-ups.

"Good God!" the doctor exclaimed. "If only I'd seen this in medical school I'd have gone into something sensible, like plumbing." Altogether, the show had an unexpectedly depressing effect. We were cheered only a little by getting our rickshaw boys to run at top speed while we hurled lighted firecrackers at people in doorways.

Heavy explosions shook the hotel early next morning. My friends of the night before were going too far, I thought, still half asleep. But then I heard the zoom of a small plane pulling out of a dive, and a short burst of aerial cannon fire, and I was wide awake and out of bed. Guns of greater caliber boomed farther away, causing the glass in the windows to shiver. By the time I got down to the lobby, the disturbance had stopped; the only signs of abnormality were that many people were already downstairs and that strangers were addressing each other in the animated, un-self-conscious manner that people assume during air raids.

"It's very bad," an old man said, shaking his head. "A picture fell off my bedroom wall. They must have come very close this time."

"Who are 'they'?" I asked. He looked at me quizzically.

"Who do you think?" he said.

"Oh, *they*—yes, of course." He must have meant the Chinese; but I had no idea, really, who was shooting at whom.

The assistant manager of the hotel, who was wearing his customary unpressed morning coat, which gave him the appearance of a disreputable undertaker, smiled unconvincingly and said aloud to himself: "Everything's all right. It is finished. They have gone away. Everything is quiet now. It is quite all right. . . ."

When the waiter served my breakfast tea (I had tried the coffee the first morning), the cup almost rattled off the saucer.

"What do you think all the shooting was about?" I asked him. He almost dropped the eggs into my lap, but recovered, looked over his shoulder and back at me and smiled and said, "It is only the harbor police, I think, checking up on illegal smugglers."

"You mean smugglers who haven't paid their dues to Dr. Lobo?" I said. The waiter winced miserably.

"Please," he begged. "I think the chef wants me. We are very busy this morning."

After breakfast I went to the Government Propaganda Section.

93

"What's all the excitement?" I asked the man on duty.

" 'Excitement'? What do you mean?" he said. In order to get a government job in Macao one must have to pass tests in poker-facedness. This man had opaque eyes. He shrugged his shoulders.

"I mean the bombs, the guns," I said.

"Oh!—these little noises! They are nothing." He snapped a finger and thumb, but silently, like a cigarette lighter that didn't work. "Pooh!" he said. "Nothing to worry about, I promise you."

"The walls of my hotel were shaken," I said.

"I don't think so," he said.

"I know so."

"Perhaps you heard the gunnery practice firing," he suggested soothingly. "The Portuguese Navy is very peaceful, but as a matter of routine occasionally there is a little shooting on the training range."

"Why didn't you say so in the first place?" I asked.

"Good sir, I assumed you know this. Everybody knows this."

In even the most delicate of situations, I have found that the best method of obtaining information is simply to ask people in a position to know what is going on. If several persons are tried, especially if they have different points of view and different interests at stake, and especially if each of them is given to believe that one has been to see the rest of them and is trying to learn the "truth," some facts usually emerge. All one needs is time, a taxi, and patience.

On this occasion, I now went to the most obvious source, the Port Captain's office, which was also Naval Headquarters. I walked briskly toward the main entrance without slackening my pace, casually saluted the sentry and said, "Good morning." In a reflex action, the sentry presented arms; and I was in.

A young Portuguese lieutenant was sitting at a desk in a reception room. He was wearing an armband; perhaps he was the officer of the day. I introduced myself by name only and asked for the operations officer. The Portuguese did not speak English. I asked him if he spoke French. A little, he said. My own French was so bad that it must have convinced him that I was from the British Consulate. I explained that I merely wanted to be shown on a large-scale chart exactly where the morning's battle had taken place.

"Oh!" the Portuguese officer said. "That is easy. I can show you myself in a moment. This way, please." He took me to a map room and showed me a wall map of Macao and the surrounding waters as far east as Hong Kong. There were some small silk flags of various colors in the sea between Macao and the mouth of the Pearl River and on some of the nearby islands. He said a Macao junk carrying cargo from Hong Kong was approaching Ladrone Island, which belonged to the Communist Chinese, when two Nationalist Chinese motor junks opened fire. Communist gunboats and shore batteries returned the fire. An unidentified aircraft attacked the Communist boats with bombs and cannon. One of the Nationalist junks was sunk. A fisherman's sampan picked up three survivors, including two wounded. The unwounded Nationalist said that twenty-six men had gone down with the boat. The second Nationalist junk was towed to Lap Sap Mei, another Communist island. The Communist losses, if any, were unknown. Was that all I wanted to know?

"What happened to the plane?"

"It flew away to the east."

"Where is the junk with the cargo for Macao?"

The Portuguese looked at his watch.

"It should arrive here very soon."

"What is the junk's name?"

He didn't know, he said; he gave me the name of the company that owned it and the address of the company's office.

"What Portuguese forces were involved?"

"None," he said. "When I said 'approaching' Ladrone Island, I did not mean 'near it.' I should say that most of the action occurred between Tai Lo and Sam Kok, here and here, Communist islands east of our island, Colowan, and about five miles beyond the territorial waters we patrol. We had no need to become involved."

I thanked him cordially and he said it was of nothing.

The manager of the import-export company that owned the Macao junk was in his office. He said that the junk had escaped unscathed. It was carrying "perfectly legal radio parts." The cargo was going north on schedule.

I went to a Western consulate. The walls of the waiting room were lined with occupied chairs. The Chinese clerk at the counter said it was quite impossible for the vice consul to see anybody more that day.

It was doubtful whether he could see all those already waiting. Perhaps if I would return early the next day. . . ? I gave him my passport and told him I had some important information for the consul. After a delay of about two minutes I was ushered into the consul's office.

"Welcome to Macao," he said, as though the words were in quotation marks. "Baltimore *Sun*. You want to know about the battle, I suppose. I'm afraid I can't tell you a thing. But why don't you join me and my wife for lunch?" He winked and nodded toward the Chinese in the outer office.

Lunch was excellent. The consular residence was typical of the colony's better homes, a spacious white house perched on a hillside overlooking the sea. There was a fresh breeze.

"That's where we hold our regattas," the consul said. "Last time one contestant's yacht turned too wide. The Chinese came out from their side and grabbed him, and we haven't seen him since. That was more than three months ago, wasn't it, dear?" he asked his wife. "Yes," he said thoughtfully. "The committee is considering altering the course."

I complimented them on their cook.

"But it gets very boring here," he said. "Everything tastes the same. The chicken's all right. But you can't get good beef. And the same dreary faces at all the parties: tennis, bridge, dances—different costumes, but the same faces. It's such a pleasure to meet someone from outside—even—ha, ha—a journalist."

"Ha, ha," I responded.

"What do you make of this morning?" he asked. "Would you like to hear my version?"

We compared notes and found that our reports were substantially the same.

"Good heavens!" the consul exclaimed. "Perhaps they were telling the truth!"

Back in the hotel, I found my room a lot tidier than I had left it. I attributed the improvement to increasingly diligent maids, until I opened my attaché case and found that someone had been looking through my notebooks. I had once read in a twenty-five-cent detective story that if one left a hair carefully draped across the pages of a book one could later detect tampering; if the snooper has not heard of the device, it works.

I wrote an account of the battle and took it to the post office, where cables were accepted. I submitted the message and my international credit card, which listed Macao, and asked how long telegraph traffic was taking to move out of the place.

"This is a very long telegram," the clerk said disapprovingly. "It will be very expensive."

"That's all right," I said. "Here's my credit card."

"You are Mr. Catling?"

"Yes."

"You will have to leave your passport."

"I prefer not to; but I'll show it to you, if you like."

"A moment, please."

He took my cable and credit card into a back room. Other customers came and went. I waited.

An older man wearing a stained gray silk tie came to the counter. "You have never before sent a telegram from Macao," he accused me.

"Everything's in order, though, isn't it?" I said.

"You are not on the list."

"What list?"

"We keep a list of persons authorized to send transferred account commercial messages."

"This is a press message," I said stiffly. "It must go quickly."

"It is not for me to say," he said. There seemed to be a gleam of pleasure in his watery eyes. I realized that it would do no good to bluster. I asked to look at my credit card.

"Look," I said, returning it together with an American five-dollar bill, folded small, "it says, 'Good for all classes of messages, including Press and Urgent Press,' and it lists Macao as a possible point of transmission. I would be most grateful if you would use your influence to get the message off without delay."

With the quick prestidigitation of a conjurer, he caused the money to disappear without apparently having noticed it.

"I will do my best," he said.

97

"I will check back in two hours," I said.

"Please, yes."

I walked along Avenida Almeida, the main shopping street, and looked into the windows, to kill time. One place was offering cheap plaster busts of Mao Tze-tung and phonograph records of Communist union songs and a paperback edition of Marx. Lee Pou-tin, a wealthy Chinese who said he had the Ford Motor Company and Coca Cola agencies for Macao, had said that Communism was a lost cause in the colony, because so many refugees had been arriving with accounts of inefficiency and discrimination in the agricultural cooperatives of China. "More and more people are turning to Chiang," Mr. Lee said. Beggars stopped me and held out their empty food bowls. One shop was selling leather holsters for revolvers. Two rickshaw boys engaged in a whining price war for my patronage. Liquor in bottles with crude counterfeit labels was expensive. "Tokyo Rose's" brother emerged abruptly from a side street and walked beside me.

"They're following you," he whispered.

"Who are?"

"It is very dangerous to help you," he said. "I have had to bribe many people."

"How much?" I asked.

"A hundred Hong Kong dollars?"

I gave him ten.

"The immigration police," he hissed, and disappeared through a wall.

The two hours had passed.

"Well," I asked the man in the post office, "has my cable gone?"

"Yes," he said. "It has gone."

"Good. When the acknowledgment arrives—I don't care what time it is—I want you to have me telephoned at the hotel. I have moved to the Grand." The Grand Hotel was small and drab and had a Chinese jazz band that played in the "ballroom" most of the night; but it was a change.

"Acknowledgment?" the man repeated.

"Yes, the acknowledgment. I have asked my office to let me know how many words they received and at what time."

"A moment, please," he said. He left the room for about five minutes.

"It is very unfortunate," he said when he returned.

"What now?"

"I am most embarrassed. The foolish clerk. He did not understand. He believed that your telegram had already been transmitted."

"You mean—"

"He threw it away. I have told him I am very cross with him."

I told him that I was pretty God-damned cross too.

"It's a good thing I made carbons," I said. "But, before I give you a copy, I must speak to the postmaster."

"I will see if he is in," the man said.

"No—I will see."

"He may be resting. It is the time of his rest."

I went behind the counter and demanded to be taken to the postmaster's office. The postmaster did not seem surprised to see me.

"Mr. Catling," he said, taking the initiative, "your telegram contains some errors. Fortunately, I was able to have it checked before they could be transmitted. If you will just sign at the end of the last page, we will be able to send the message without delay."

He handed me my cable, which was now barely recognizable. Many words had been obliterated with red crayon.

"A formality," he said with an unctuous smile. "If you will just sign, please."

"Where is the censor? I wasn't told about any censorship," I protested.

"There is no censorship," the postmaster said. "But of course it would be unfortunate for all concerned if pressmen sent false information from Macao. It is our job to help you."

"Are you or are you not going to send this cable as I wrote it?" I asked.

"Please be reasonable," the postmaster said.

I snatched the cable from his hand and left his office.

Two swarthy Portuguese in dark brown suits came to their feet in the lobby of the Grand Hotel when I got back.

"Mr. Catling?" one said.

"We have good news for you," said the other. "We have succeeded in expediting your Nationalist visa."

"But—" I said.

"If you will please come with us to the office of the chief of police," said the first.

"Come, please," said the other, gently but firmly leading me by one arm.

A fat man in a white suit and sunglasses received me at police headquarters. Tea was brought in. I refused it. He offered me a cigar. I refused it.

"Now, Mr. Catling," he said genially. "I understand that your papers are in good order. The Nationalist representative informs us that he has made a special effort to help you visit his country. You may obtain your visa at any time—immediately, in fact."

I said that was good.

"You American newspapermen are always in such a hurry," he said with a tolerant smile. "I suppose you will be leaving Macao very soon."

"Quite soon, I suppose."

"We might be able to help you secure a first-class place aboard tonight's steamer," the police chief said. "However, you might prefer to sail tomorrow morning." His smile faded. "With your friend Mr. O'Brien in the *Lee Hong*."

"That sounds very tempting," I said. "If only I felt sure that the shooting had come to an end here."

"Mr. Catling," the police chief said (or the man who seemed to be the police chief; fraudulence was making me dizzy). "Permit me to be very frank. We have been disturbed by what you have written. Frankly, a copy of your telegram was sent to this office. In this telegram there were many false statements. You said that explosions have been shaking your hotel. This cannot be true. This morning there was a small incident, but it was far away; it was nearer to Hong Kong than to Macao. It does not concern us here. In Macao, everything is peaceful. We have good relations with all nations. We do not want to alarm anybody. If somebody tells you false rumors and you send them to your newspaper, some people may be led to false conclusions about the situation here."

"Doesn't the Portuguese Navy know what's going on?" I asked. The police chief's face darkened ominously.

"This foolish young officer to whom you talked without permission has been reprimanded. He was a very junior officer. He has been here a short time. He does not understand the situation. He wanted to make you think he was important, that he knew everything. He knows nothing about the disposition of ships. It is not his job to know. He has only a junior administrative job. What he told you was wrong. The Chinese are most careful to avoid unnecessary naval activities. If there was any shooting it was probably directed against smugglers only."

"Perhaps you're right," I said; "perhaps I should get back to Hong Kong."

"You may write any fairy stories you like in Hong Kong," the chief of police said. "Many crazy stories are written there. Nobody who knows anything believes them. But we do not want such stories written in Macao."

"You won't mind if I report that the Government of Macao has imposed censorship on the American press," I said.

"I have said nothing about censorship. You will have to speak to other authorities about that."

The next morning I sailed for Hong Kong. In the *Lee Hong* I gave O'Brien some genuine French-type brandy. The day after that I took off for Taipei. It was not until weeks later that I discovered that the cable I had written in Macao had been largely de-censored and transmitted to Baltimore. Perhaps the "other authorities" in Macao had more sense of proportion than some of the people I had dealt with. Anyway, the articles about Macao published in the Baltimore *Sun* caused no perceptible stir whatsoever.

18

When I arrived in the Formosan capital in February, 1953, it was quite obvious that the Nationalists' new freedom to try to realize their slogan, "Back to the Mainland," was embarrassing them. President Chiang was trying to climb down from his militant posture without losing face, as a man poised on a high diving board might climb down as soon as the pool is filled, with the explanation that he believes that his water wings need a bit more inflation.

Macao had been dreamlike enough; but commerce, legitimate and illegitimate, had been a link with reality. Taipei's only apparent connection with the real world was American aid; and the money and technical assistance from the United States only prolonged the vain, delusive prophecy that one day the Nationalists would return triumphantly to China. But in those days Washington strategists were still thinking in terms of the "surface containment" of Communism; all sentimentality aside, a majority of United States Congressmen evidently thought that to pay President Chiang—Generalissimo Chiang—to maintain his forces on Formosa was a worthwhile investment; if Chiang's aging infantrymen did not continue to drill and maneuver, the Communist perimeter in the Orient might move a hundred miles and more to the east. While nuclear weapons were being withheld from the Korean War the threat of nuclear bombing alone was not considered sufficient to deter the Communists from attacking Formosa. Formosa itself had to be strong—or had to seem strong.

The Nationalist Ministry of Public Enlightenment thus had the difficult task of persuading foreign journalists, especially American journalists, that Formosa, with American aid, was strong enough to withstand invasion, and almost—but not quite—strong enough to invade. To be strong enough to return to the mainland, the Nationalist Government would need many more millions of dollars and more time. The Nationalists have been saying the same ever since.

Chinese information officers with California and New York accents courteously informed me of the interviews that would be arranged for me during my stay.

"This is open house," one said with a comprehensive gesture. "We will show you everything."

I was glad, when I walked back to the Friends of China Club where I was staying, to find that I would not be without companionship during the trying days ahead. In the bar before lunch I found John Ridley, in a ginger tweed hacking jacket and cavalry twill trousers, sipping a pink gin. I was delighted. I was also amazed, and I must have shown it.

"What are you doing here?" I asked.

He knew what I meant, evidently; he replied rather pettishly: "The same as you, I imagine. You mustn't believe the slanderers who say that I spend all my time in the Seoul press billets. I get about. As a matter of fact, I have come to talk to George Yeh, a dear friend." Dr. Yeh was the Foreign Minister. "He read for his M.A. at Cambridge, you know. I'll introduce you to him, if you wish. But first shall we have just one tiny drink before lunch? The food here is, of course, abominable."

While we were picking disconsolately at cold meat, a messenger came to our table, presented Ridley with a small envelope, and waited, apparently expecting a reply.

Oh, dear," Ridley said wearily. "They are such awful bores. I'm sure they mean well; one gives them the benefit of the doubt; but how they do go on! This boy keeps coming over all day with his tiresome chits. This one's an invitation to an interview with a Point Four agrologist. Really! I ask you! Young man, please return to the Ministry of Public Enlightenment, and tell the director that Mr. Ridley is most appreciative, but he really doesn't want another talk about the rice yield." Ridley turned to me and said: "If I hear another word about tons of rice per hectare I think I'll go right off my rocker. I don't even know what a hectare is, do you? It isn't in the back of *my* diary. Why can't they tell us these things in acres, if they must tell us at all? Why must they tell us at all? What are they trying to prove? Why *must* they be so inscrutable?"

"Mr. Lee said, if you cannot come at 2:30, please come at three o'clock," the messenger insisted. "He said you should bring Mr. Catling, too. Mr. Lee said the interview is arranged. Mr. Lee said it is important. Mr. Lee said he will soon arrange an interview with Dr. Yeh."

"You see," Ridley said. "They've got us where they want us, and they know it. No Point Four, no foreign affairs. If you want one, you've got to have both. That's the way it works."

"Surely—"

"No, it's no use. I've tried. There's no getting out of it. You may as well come with me now. If you don't come now they'll make you come another day before they give you anything you really want."

So we went and heard a long lecture on chemical fertilizers and rice yields, complete with two-year-old statistics.

The Ministry of Public Enlightenment reported that secret agents in Hong Kong had learned that the Communist administration of Chungshan, a Cantonese provincial subdivision, had ordered compulsory marriage for all eligible widows between the ages of twenty and fifty-five, women whose husbands had been overseas for three years or more, women whose husbands were impotent, and concubines and waitresses.

"What's the point of this release?" I asked Ridley.

"The bit about women whose husbands have been overseas for

more than three years—wives of Nationalists who are now on Formosa, for example."

"That'll be rather hard on Nationalist Army morale, won't it?" I suggested.

"I should think so, yes, very," Ridley agreed.

"Wouldn't it have been wiser for the Nationalists to have kept this bit of news dark then?"

"Inscrutability," Ridley said.

Ridley and I were sent by train to Tso Ying to witness the invasion training of 6,000 Chinese marines. A seventy-two-man U.S. Marine Corps amphibious warfare instruction team demonstrated invasion techniques with toys on an outdoor basketball court. The audience included numerous Nationalist officers.

"Ah," sighed a Nationalist naval captain. "If only we had battleships and aircraft carriers."

"I can see that our artillery is quite obsolete," remarked a Nationalist colonel of infantry.

"What can we hope to achieve before we receive sufficient bombs of modern potency?" asked a Nationalist air force general.

We were granted an audience with the Foreign Minister.

"The basic requirements for retaking the mainland are not yet in sight," he said.

The Ministry of Public Enlightenment sent Ridley and me invitations to a reception in the Government Guest House for Martin Artajo, the Foreign Minister of Spain, who had flown to Formosa to proclaim the solidarity of the governments of Madrid and Taipei.

Several American priests, refugees from the mainland, had been invited to the party, presumably to give it a Catholic appearance. One by one they approached us to ask if there was anything we could do to bring world opinion to bear against Chiang Ching-kuo, the Generalissimo's Moscow-trained son. They said his secret police and commissars were campaigning ruthlessly against Christian teaching in the Nationalist armed services and schools. People could not be loyal to the Kuomintang and to Christianity at the same time, young Chiang had said.

"This place is beginning to suffocate me," I said. "I think I'll go somewhere else to write about it."

"I'm glad to hear that," Ridley said. "I feared that I was being influenced merely by acute feelings of homesickness."

"Homesickness? But you haven't tried to get to your home in England for years, have you?"

"I don't mean homesickness for Northumberland," he said. "I'm homesick for Seoul. I miss Yao."

"The trouble is that I still have quite a wad of Nationalist dollars. The manager of the club says the black market won't change them back."

"You buy the tickets then," Ridley suggested. "I'll pay you in Seoul in champagne."

"I'll still have about sixty dollars over."

"Sixty *Nationalist* dollars? You can get your trousers pressed and your shoes shined," Ridley said.

19

Partly because Patrick O'Donovan had been able to save my room, adjoining his, in the best available suite in the press billets, and partly because it was to our mutual advantage to share the costs of a domestic staff (I was trying to hold my expenses down to $250 a week), on my return to Seoul one of my first jobs was to help O'Donovan find an interpreter we both liked.

We already had a part-time houseboy and a communal laundry-woman who washed clothing every day; and the Army provided a maid to make the beds and to dust the rooms.

The boy arrived every morning at about seven o'clock, on his way to school. He was about fifteen years old and very shy, which we thought was a good thing for him to be at that hour. His duties were to clear up what was left of the food and drink and wash the dishes and glasses and throw away the débris from the night before, to polish our shoes, and to put a kettle of water on the spirit stove for our early morning tea. The theory was that he would have finished these chores in time for him to get to school before the bell, and that the noise of the boiling kettle would wake O'Donovan shortly before eight o'clock, giving us a chance to put in a long and active day covering the war. What actually happened was that O'Donovan turned off the kettle without fully awakening. We usually made a more serious attempt to start the day soon after the arrival of the maid.

The maid was a good woman who worked hard and earned our unqualified respect, but she had two attributes that made it difficult to enjoy her daily visits: she wore canoe-shaped white rubber shoes that squished and squelched internally as she walked around the rooms; and she exuded and exhaled the overwhelming odor of *kimshi*, the Korean national dish, which contains a lot of cabbage and garlic. When I heard the scrape and knock of O'Donovan's Japanese wooden sandals hurrying away down the stone passage to the showers I realized that the maid had arrived; and, sure enough, within a few minutes her squashy sounds and *kimshi* aura entered my room and got me also to my feet and my ablutions. We usually finished shaving and dressing in time to call on Ridley for drinks before lunch.

As far as it went, this staff was quite satisfactory; however, both O'Donovan and I, while recognizing the primacy of the United Nations in Korea as far as news was concerned, were disinclined to emulate the majority of our colleagues in ignoring the Koreans except in terms of ROK divisions. And in order to learn about the Koreans as people it was necessary to be able to talk to them—any of them, not only the relatively few who spoke some English. A friendly reporter on the *Chosen Ilbo* said that well qualified Korean-English interpreters were easy to find; he advised inserting an advertisement in his own newspaper, one of the most respected in South Korea. An advertisement was composed and published; it was one column wide and about an inch deep.

We wondered whether there would be any response.

The morning the advertisement appeared there was a faint tap on the door after the boy had gone to school and before the arrival of the laundrywoman or the maid.

"God!" O'Donovan protested. "What is it?"

There was a moment's silence, and then another tap.

"It must be for you," O'Donovan shouted.

"I'm not expecting anyone," I shouted back. "Maybe it's a new messenger, who doesn't know that handouts are supposed to be put on the floor."

Another tap.

"A reader of Poe," I suggested.

"Well, if you haven't the decency to see who it is," O'Donovan said, "even though I happen to have a frightful headache. . . ."

"I happen to have one too," I replied. "Anyway, the door's in your room; answering the door is a price you have to pay for having taken the bigger room while my back was turned."

There was another tap. It was like the Chinese water torture.

"Oh, all right, all right," O'Donovan grumbled. "I'm coming." He got up, donned his *yukata* (summer kimono) and sunglasses and went to the door.

"The least you can do," he shouted at me before opening it, "is to make the bloody tea for a change."

The door opened to admit a frail, elderly Korean in a white linen suit that looked yellow with age, like paper. His skin was like antique parchment. He wore silver-rimmed pince-nez spectacles and carried in two hands, like an offering, his hat, a Panama with a mournful black band.

"Mr. O'Donovan?" the Korean asked in a voice that quavered with uncertainty.

O'Donovan, who had realized at last that this man must be an applicant for the interpreting job, stared at him with an expression of mingled consternation and pity.

"Yes," O'Donovan admitted.

"I have read in *Chosen Ilbo* today your advertisement, sir," the man said with a ghastly, strained smile. "May I be permitted to offer my services, sir. I have letters of reference." He thrust a trembling, bony hand inaccurately into his jacket and fumbled for the pocket.

"No, no," O'Donovan said. "I mean, yes, of course. It's very good of you to have come. Do have something to drink—would you like a cup of tea?"

The Korean produced a Manila envelope, from which, with exquisite care, he extracted several wrinkled letters that had been fortified with strips of adhesive paper along the folds.

"As well as English and German, including scientific German," the Korean said, "I speak fluently the Mandarin dialect of China, sir, where I have taught for many years before the war." He was already speaking more freely and a bit too animatedly, in the manner of an unsuccessful salesman who expects failure but wants to prolong the conversation for the sake of postponing rejection.

I placed two cups of tea on O'Donovan's massive, richly carved Korean desk. It had cost only about 4,000 hwan ($20) in a local secondhand furniture store, but it added a substance and authority to the room that made the Korean seem like a ghost. The teacups were quite ordinary Japanese pottery, but were decorated with such subtle colors and delicate simplicity of design and were so highly glazed that they made him look all the drabber and poorer. And, being Japanese, they had no handles; the tea was very hot; the Korean found that he was unable to hold his cup, and smiled another miserable smile. O'Donovan apologetically put down his own cup; and I, a helpless bystander, turned in embarrassment to potter about aimlessly with utensils in the sink.

O'Donovan told the Korean that his qualifications sounded very high, indeed too high for the simple, unimportant job that had to be done; we needed only a simple interpreter; an inexperienced man would be adequate. The more awkward the conversation became, the more brightly the Korean smiled. O'Donovan suggested that a learned scholar such as the applicant would really be wasting his time in such an unworthy, mechanical job. And, finally (an inspiration), we couldn't allow him to expose himself to the risks that would be entailed in journeys under gunfire at the front. And the Korean smiled and smiled, until I felt like begging him to stop. O'Donovan ceremoniously wrote down the Korean's name and asked for his address. Of course, he had no address. He said it didn't matter; he might soon be getting an academic appointment in Taegu; he wasn't sure where he would be staying in the meantime; perhaps we could reach him, if we wished, through the *Chosen Ilbo*. He would keep in touch with the paper. He was grateful for having been received. He was grateful for the tea (untouched). He was grateful, he suggested, for the privilege of having breathed the air of our honorable quarters. He withdrew backward, and then sideways, and then turned and walked away quickly, as though relieved that the suspense was over, that the glimpse of impossible luxury, the private rooms, the desk and the teacups, was behind him.

"How terrible," O'Donovan said. "His suit! Did you notice how carefully the trousers had been pressed? The exquisite darns? The buttons that didn't exactly match? The tightness of the jacket? It was the most pathetic suit in the world. How frightful that anyone should want a job so badly—and look at you!"

"I want a job," I said defensively. "I mean, I appreciate mine. Well, I mean, I was sorry for him, too. But he really wouldn't have done, would he? He was far too old and decrepit. You know what I mean."

"You're jolly well going to interview the next one, if there is one," O'Donovan said.

"Why on earth didn't we give him some money?" I asked.

"He wouldn't have taken it. I didn't think of it. It was too awful."

"Let's have a drink."

"Yes: a delicious gin and Kia-Ora lemon squash, please, in a small glass, like a drink in a theater bar."

"Yes," I said. "Let's pretend he wasn't real."

But there was another tap on the door.

The dismal, threadbare parade went on and on. Most of the men were actually late middle-aged, or looked it, or were obviously physically handicapped, or were flashy, sleek young men who evidently assumed that because we were war correspondents we must be trying to establish contact with the black market.

We eventually hired a young Korean Army lieutenant who had recently been given a medical discharge. He wore an American uniform without insignia or badges of rank. He said he had been a student at Seoul University before the war. He spoke English with a slight American accent. He was respectful without being obsequious. He said he wanted a job because he could not support his wife on his military pension. We offered him $20 a week. He considered the offer with an apparent lack of enthusiasm. He explained his reluctance by pointing out that $20 a week would be six times as much as the salary paid to General Paik Sun Yup, the ROK Army chief of staff. He felt that it would be improper for a former lieutenant to receive more than his former commanding officer. We argued that General Paik had free army housing and food and transportation and certain special perquisites that made up for the disparity in cash. The lieutenant accepted the offer. We suggested that he should report to us six days a week to find out whether his services were required. He said that he would come every day, because Korean soldiers had no holidays. We allowed him to report every day.

It was difficult to think of things for him to do. He arrived each morning, a visible conscience, silently reproaching us for not having thought of Koreans to interview. I began to get up early in order to be dressed before his arrival. He looked pained whenever we dismissed him without work. He said that it seemed wrong that he should be paid so much for idleness. That was the newspaper game, I explained. Dutifully O'Donovan and I went on a few visits to Korean Government departments, though President Rhee was such a masterful despot that interviews with his inferiors lacked authority and were of limited value. We visited the West Gate Prison and were taken into the execution hut in which, we were told, Japanese soldiers had executed many prisoners during World War II. Were many executions taking place now? "Yes," said the director of the prison with a broad grin. He held out a noose playfully and invited me to try it on. "Number one for newspaper writer," he said.

I visited the head offices of ROK veterans' associations, formed to try to help veterans of the army, navy, air force, and marine corps and their families to survive in the penury that ordinarily followed discharge. The pension then being paid was the equivalent of sixty dollars a year. Because of inflation, the average family could not subsist in a city for less than about fifty dollars a month. Koreans were unable to save money while they served in their armed forces; a private was paid about thirty-five cents a month.

Our interpreter seemed to derive satisfaction from helping to bring facts of this kind to the attention of American and British newspaper readers. I wrote several stories about the plight of Korean civilians. If there was ever any reaction to these stories I never heard anything about it; however, CARE packages were coming into the country, and not all the recipients sold them on the black market.

After a short time, we tired of the interpreter's laborious oral reports of what the Korean newspapers were saying. We got him to prepare a daily written press summary. He typed it with two fingers on O'Donovan's typewriter. This procedure consumed several hours a day. It was occasionally useful to us and it seemed to keep the interpreter happy. After a month or so of this drudgery he was willing to accept a few cans of food to take home to his wife.

O'Donovan closely scrutinized himself in the mirror on the wall, a small, circular shaving mirror that distorted the dimensions of the face, elongating or broadening it as one raised or lowered it. One could never be sure which was the true image and which the distortion.

"The world's greatest journalist," he observed, a trifle wearily; the burden of superlative greatness *was* wearisome. In fact, on good days, he really was, in my opinion, the greatest. Second greatest, anyway. He was not a devotee of the cult of objectivity, at whose hollow shrine most of the rest of us, with varying degrees of sincerity, did regular obeisance. This modern school of journalism, which has reached its most extreme development in the more respectable newspapers of the United States, is governed by the principle that expressions of opinion belong on the editorial page and there only, that a newspaper's news columns must be untainted by personalities. A perfectly impartial, unbiased, objective news article would present every relevant fact about any given subject without any particular point of view, or focus, or emphasis. Ideally, every fact would be presented simultaneously, in order to avoid the greater and lesser impacts of precedence and succession. Ideally, the facts would have been gathered not by one man only but by an infinitely large, infinitely wise committee of people who were of this world, yet above its prejudices and passions and vested interests. The standards of genuine total objectivity are superhuman; language itself is practically incapable of attaining them, for words mean different things to different men; there is no way of purging words of their emotive accretions: even the most coldly scientific of articles in the most Olympian of medical journals is a-twitch and a-twitter with emotional connotations. But many conscientious journalists, overlooking the subjectivity of their initial decisions about what story to cover, where to go for it, what to look at, whom to listen to, and what observations to record and what to discard, mix pro and con and black and white, fifty-fifty, write it all as flatly as they possibly can, and believe that the dull gray monochrome they produce is objectivity. The objectivist's self-deception or hypocrisy often becomes obvious by the time the "objective" reporter's opus has undergone "objective" editing and copyreading and has been published in a particular place under "objective" headlines on a particular page, above or below or beside other "objective" stories, and near or not near relevant or irrelevant photographs and drawings. There is so much interaction between the elements of any story and between it and its surroundings that not even the dullest, blandest, grayest monochrome can disguise the fact that the whole fabrication is human handiwork from beginning to end, and not in any respect impersonal, let alone godly.

O'Donovan was fortunate in not having to try to seem objective. He was openly, eloquently subjective, personal, himself, idiosyncratic, stating opinions, offering judgments, using adjectives and adverbs as flagrantly adjectivally and adverbially as he pleased. Having talent, knowledge and experience, he was qualified to do so; and he had as much sympathy, acuity of perception and felicity of expression in his little finger as there seemed to be in a whole bureauful of "objective" wire-service hacks. In fairness or semifairness to them, it must be added that O'Donovan was writing first and foremost for a single newspaper published once a week, and only secondly, now and then, for papers that subscribed to the *Observer* foreign service. He could allow himself the rare journalistic luxuries of premeditation and fastidiousness. He could sit in a yoga knot, in a mystic trance, contemplating a void, if he chose to, awaiting the internal formulation of an exact, a perfect, phrase, the revelation of a *mot juste*, in the time that I, at my assembly line in the next room, was obliged to hammer out five hundred phrases that were not quite precise, that were short of perfection, and that only occasionally were approximately *juste*.

Our tempos were different. My temperamental crises were frequent and superficial; the cycle of his moods was weekly, a slow revolution from the perigee of despondency, near deadline, to the apogee of exultation, on the day that clippings arrived which showed, with a regularity that I began to find tedious, that he was doing spectacularly well. But even when there was no rational reason for anxiety, O'Donovan, like most of the newspapermen I have known who care about their writing as writing, suffered from fear of literary impotence.

"Listen to this," he would say, in the full flush of a soirée, with the room full of correspondents of various nationalities. "I want to read a particularly beautiful sentence." Absolute silence was mandatory, on pain of expulsion. Then he would read, in his BBC Third Program recitative voice, a good sentence from his latest published article. "Isn't it beautiful?" he would ask. "Isn't it? Am I not the greatest journalist in the world?" A newcomer, unaware of the house rules, might make some casual, flippant comment, and O'Donovan's morale, the house of cards that had been erected so painstakingly, would collapse in disorder. "No. You're right. It's no use. I'll never write another line." Laughter, rash laughter, burst out.

"All right," O'Donovan exploded, "that's the end! You're all quite impossible. No, I cannot tolerate you. You'll all have to leave. Out, all of you, out; and never, never come back!"

O'Donovan then swept off his desk a few glasses, as an earnest of his intention to destroy the entire press billets, if necessary, to achieve immediate solitude. Then as the indignant guests left, muttering, grumbling, the light was snapped out and we silently retired.

The following night the same guests would return as though nothing had happened, and O'Donovan, having written during the interim something worth while, would graciously forgive those who had trespassed against him, and demonstrate the restoration of his good humor by standing on a table and singing Sinn Fein rebel songs to the beat of his stamping *geta*.

20

The British Commonwealth Division occupied a sector of the Western Front athwart what was referred to as "the historic Seoul invasion route." The British Army and associated units were conveniently near us, as well as being in action as often as other units, and more often than some; and it was a hospitable division.

O'Donovan decided to do an article on the Royal Artillery. He already knew a good deal about the principles and practices of British gunners, I learned, because he had been an officer in a tank regiment of the Irish Guards in the British Army throughout World War II. Now, in Korea, he added to his improvised uniform a Brigade of Guards cap, which has a Prussian arrogance about its vertical front, with a high top and a visor that almost covers the eyes. He said that he would have to insist thenceforward on a little more respect.

"You will address me as Major O'Donovan," he said. Annoyingly enough, his rank was two degrees above what mine had been, so it was no use to try to counter his new affectation in kind. I could do only the opposite: when we set off in a jeep for the British press camp, I wore a Japanese tropical-worsted shirt and trousers, leather bedroom slippers and a Korean rice-straw sombrero.

"I had never before actually believed all that I had heard of Air Force slovenliness," he commented, trying not to seem jealous as he stared at the straw hat, which was, I am willing to admit, a touch of genius.

The British public relations officer who received us at division headquarters was a striking example of War Office carelessness about matching a man's inclinations and skills to his job. He felt loathing for the press which he hardly concealed. He was a quiet, gentle, rather stuffy man who wanted only to be left alone so that he could exercise his sole talent, an aptitude for sighting, capturing, and classifying butterflies.

"What do you want to do here?" he asked us apprehensively.

"Nothing," O'Donovan said. "Simply visit some people for a day or two. All we want from you is somewhere to sleep. I thought I might do something on the Gunners. Catling here, I suppose—well, he's from the Baltimore *Sun*."

"I wanted to visit the Black Watch before they go to Kenya to fight the Mau-Mau."

"There's nothing been said on that," the PRO told me sharply. "Where did you hear it?"

"Someone in Seoul. He said he'd always thought the Black Watch was an Ethiopian sentry."

"Nothing has been released," the PRO insisted.

"Then I'll do something else. What do you recommend?"

"Oh, stop fussing, Catling," O'Donovan said. "Do the Gunners. 'The beautiful precision of mathematics: death by slide rule, etc.' They may shoot for us."

As we were being led to our tent, O'Donovan earnestly said: "By the way. . . . Before we go up to the line. . . ."

"Yes?"

"Really, you can't wear that hat. In the Brigade. . . ."

"I'll throw it away on one condition."

"What's that?"

"You stop saying 'in the Brigade.' "

The hat was thrown away; but O'Donovan did not stick to his part of the bargain.

British officers' messes in Korea were generous to a fault with afterdinner brandy.

The night was cold and dark. The jeep's dim blue blackout lights revealed the narrow track only a few feet ahead. O'Donovan's Gregorian chanting detracted not at all from my sense of insecurity. Eventually, however, we got back all right to our tent. It was an eight-man tent; but that night we were the only visiting correspondents.

"It's freezing," I pointed out.

"Wear your socks in bed," O'Donovan suggested.

"But I do anyway."

"How revolting."

"I wish I had an electric blanket."

"Effete Americans."

"You're the man who wanted to send his linen ahead to the Marines," I reminded him.

"If you don't know the difference, one can't explain."

Drowsily, the bickering continued. Too drowsily, I felt. There had been cases of asphyxiation in overheated tents. There was a rule that the cylindrical oilstove in the center of the tent had to be damped at night. The heat-control dial, calibrated from 1 to 9, was supposed to be set at 1, no matter what the outside temperature was.

"You haven't turned up the stove?" I asked.

"Uh?"

"The stove—have you turned it up?"

"No. Have you?"

"I haven't touched it."

"Nor have I."

I noticed that the interior of the tent was not totally dark. There was a faint glow of light. I wondered if I were dreaming.

"It seems to be getting lighter," I said.

"What is it now?"

"Oh, nothing. . . . O'Donovan, is the stovepipe supposed to glow red like that?"

"It isn't red; it's orange."

"It's cherry red."

"Nonsense—orange."

"Now it's getting orange," I conceded. "It wasn't orange when I first looked. It was red."

"Oh, do shut up and go to sleep."

"It was cherry red."

Now the glow was spreading. The whole stovepipe became bright pale orange.

"You must have forgotten to turn the stove down," O'Donovan said. I could see across the narrow floor that he was propped up on one elbow looking up at the pipe. I could feel its heat on my forehead.

"Since when have I been responsible for adjusting stoves?" I asked.

"The last man into bed is expected to turn the stove down."

"Ha. But I happened to get to bed first."

"You'd better do something about it. It's yellow. It must be getting damned hot."

"I'm not getting up. It's taken all this time to get my toes unfrozen."

"Go on—don't be an oaf."

"Why don't you?"

"Look," O'Donovan said in a milder tone of voice. "It really is rather splendid, isn't it? It'll soon be white."

"It couldn't turn white. It's still quite a dark yellow really. It's just the contrast with the darkness that makes it seem almost white."

"Don't be absurd. I've got eyes. It's white."

These were two reporters arguing about what they could see. Their reports were part of the free world's effort in what had been called the global battle for men's minds.

We argued until the top of the tent actually burst into flames of all hues of red and yellow and the intermediate mixtures—a Viking pyre, a miniature volcano in eruption.

We got everything out all right, including a flask of whisky, which we passed to and fro as we leaned against the jeep and watched the dark canvas consumed. There was nothing that could be done to save it. The PRO had some camp beds set up in the mess.

"I suppose I'll have to write a report on this," the PRO said halfheartedly over bacon and eggs next morning.

"Then we'd better not be getting back to Seoul," O'Donovan said. "We'll have to stay until everything's cleared up. In the Brigade. . . ."

For once I did not mind his saying it, because when he did a look of horror came into the PRO's eyes. He probably foresaw the interminable paperwork, the official questions and answers, the court of inquiry, that might result if a report of the incident suggested that we had been grossly negligent and if O'Donovan insisted on a chance formally to try to clear himself. The PRO probably foresaw a lot of days spent not chasing rare Korean butterflies.

"I don't want to hold you chaps up with a lot of red tape," he said magnanimously. "I imagine the stove was defective. A lot of them are. I'm sure the tent can be written off without a lot of bother for you."

On the way back to Seoul, O'Donovan and I both commented that it was fortunate that the other's stubbornness had not resulted in major embarrassment. I made one concession.

"All things considered, that cap of yours is probably an asset."

"It was probably just as well that you're from the Baltimore *Sun*," O'Donovan responded courteously. "After all, most of the tents that get burned in this country are American ones. It was the least we could do to let you burn one of ours."

The next time we went up to the Commonwealth Division press camp was for O'Donovan's St. Patrick's Day party, which, it was generally agreed, was the social high light of the season.

Tables were ranged lengthwise along two sides of the mess tent as a bar and a buffet. There was a prodigious quantity of NAAFI food and drink, augmented by delicacies such as smoked salmon, smoked oysters, and caviar, which were specially flown over from Tokyo. O'Donovan had sent out formal invitations ("Carriages at Three O'clock"), which filled the tent with generals, including a group of bewildered Canadians from Ottawa who had arrived in Korea only the day before for a quick inspection tour of the battle zone and had expected rigors.

The Black Watch sent over some pipers in full dress uniforms. They swaggered superbly in small circles around the stove and inflated the tent with the heroic, vibrant, nasal scream of Scottish martial music. They concluded the exhilarating concert with the newest addition to their ancient regimental repertoire, "Arirang," a traditional Korean air, melodically similar to, and as plaintive as, "Over the Sea to Skye."

John Ridley demonstrated his fortitude and grace as a matador, adding substance to accounts of his activities in Spain. The captain who had spent the night with O'Donovan and me in the Japanese hotel played fervently the part of the bull, using two quart bottles of Asahi beer as horns. In one headlong charge that was confused in the daringly late swirl of Ridley's tablecloth cape, the bull collided heavily with the stove, and another incineration seemed imminent; but the stovepipe was straightened successfully and the party continued unabated, unspoiled even when the commanding general of the Commonwealth Division, in the throes of jitterbugging, painfully wrenched the shoulder of a young lady in the uniform of one of the United Nations' relief agencies. The mishap caused widespread consternation, partly because she was one of very few women present. A medical officer, who had not been wholly abstemious during the past several hours, examined her there and then and declared her A-1, and she went on dancing almost as uninhibitedly as before.

All these festivities took place within range of Chinese artillery. If the enemy had known of the extraordinary concentration of high-ranking British officers and journalists in that tent that night, a single accurate shell might have wrought havoc in Whitehall, if not in Fleet Street.

"We don't want to believe it," as Stephen Barber, of the London *News Chronicle*, pointed out; "it's hard to accept; but the fact is that we're all expendable, all of us. None of our papers, in America or England, would have the slightest difficulty in replacing any of us within a week."

The thought was a sobering one, but not too. It was a very, very good party.

21

Spring sunshine melted the ice on the rice paddies. The khaki landscape was softened with patches of green. The buds of wild azaleas opened on the foothills. Mud turned to dust. The colors became Provençal. The sky, the mountains and the cubistic flat planes of agricultural terraces resembled paintings by Cézanne.

I encountered a GI graves registrar or interment supervisor close to the front shortly after a Chinese attack. He had been given the job of burying Chinese. I believe Koreans did the actual digging. He was a very young man, a high-grade hillbilly with a blank, tan face and unclouded eyes. He had been drafted from an apprenticeship in his home-town mortuary. He wasn't complaining, he said; it had happened to lots of fellers, being taken away from civilian life, just when they were getting ahead good. He always looked on the bright side; he guessed he had been kind of lucky.

An Army truck groaned up the hill and dumped a load of fresh corpses. They were arranged in neat rows under a tarpaulin shelter.

122

"At least I get to do something that helps me keep up with my trade," he said. "We're too busy, of course, to handle the cadavers the way we would at home. Anyway, we're not supposed to fix them up fancy. But still it's better than nothing. We get all kinds, in all kinds of conditions. What I do is I look them over good, and figure out what they need, what I'd do if they belonged to clients. I've learned a lot, just imagining what I'd do. It's been right interesting."

I left him happily whistling between his teeth as he totted up the day's score.

Michael Rougier, a *Life* photographer who got as close to the war as anyone possibly could have got to it, reacted to death and destruction in an inspired way: he started building an electric model railroad.

Having got his films off to the airport, he used to spend many evenings in the press billets, tinkering with small-scale Japanese locomotives and freight cars. He built tracks on planks and had a Korean carpenter attach them to brackets chest-high along the walls of his bedroom. As more trains came over from Tokyo, he found that the railroad was getting cramped, so he had tunnels chiseled through the walls. The railroad expanded.

A man who lived in one of the rooms next to Rougier's said it was weird, but not unpleasant, late at night, to hear the tiny wail of a Rougier Diesel, and to see the glow from its headlight as it emerged from the tunnel.

Barber, when he was not painting baroque murals in the billets, and I took our own toys to the British Officers' Club, in Seoul, which had tennis courts, bowling alleys, a bar, and a swimming pool. We specialized in model ships. As I had just spent a few days aboard the U.S.S. *Oriskany*, an aircraft carrier, part of Task Force 77 in the Sea of Japan, I was posing at that time as a naval authority. Barber and I played with various surface vessels amicably enough. But one day in a Tokyo toyshop he found some submarines. Submarine warfare brought out the worst in both of us. One afternoon Barber's submarine dived and failed to come up again. The water in the pool was murky, not having been changed for three or four weeks. (It was changed only when the American officer in charge of local fire-fighting equipment felt like a swim.) Sunken objects could be retrieved only by diving and groping for them. Barber abandoned his submarine with angry accusations of enemy sabotage, though I vehemently denied the charge; and relations between us seemed rather strained for some months.

The day it was announced that the first contingent of sick and wounded United Nations prisoners of war were on their way from North Korean prison camps to be exchanged at Panmunjom with Communist prisoners from the south, I asked Lieutenant General Glen O. Barcus, commanding general of the United States Fifth Air Force, whether it would be possible to fly north for an aerial preview of the first convoy of ambulances.

"When do you want to leave?" was the general's only question. The USAF, in Korea as elsewhere, did not mess about with public relations: it did things fast and it did them in a big way: the next morning I was provided with a Shooting Star (a two-place jet trainer) and an escort of five Sabrejets for my private sightseeing tour. The size of the escort was so impressive that I wasn't even too upset by the name of the pilot who was assigned to fly the Shooting Star— Captain Coffin.

An Air Force photographer took some photographs of me in flying suit and helmet beside the plane. I felt like a celebrity in a night club. It was difficult to tell who was supposed to be publicizing whom.

The Sabres were already orbiting protectively overhead, and their fuel consumption was prodigious, so Captain Coffin dismissed the photographer. He took just two more shots of me sitting in the plane, with my molars clamped together in a way that I hoped would suggest *Hell's Angels.*

The wing of the Shooting Star dipped like a diviner's wand and pointed to the convoy. It looked like a caravan of matchboxes, moving slowly along the tortuous, bomb-pitted North Korean road. We flew over Pyongyang, the Communist capital. A man in a field waved. Then we were near the forbidden Yalu River. I saw two condensation trails, like two chalk lines on a blue ceiling, high above us, moving southward from the direction of the MIG bases.

We turned about and headed home in a shallow dive. The Shooting Star flies slower than sound, and the plane started buffeting as we approached the sound barrier. Captain Coffin pulled the nose up and I felt the bladders of my G-suit dilate unpleasantly and my helmet press leadenly down on my eyes. Once we were south of the 38th parallel, Captain Coffin seemed to relax.

"Would you like some aerobatics?" he asked. I felt that I had to say I would. He performed some sickeningly smooth barrel rolls, Cuban eights, Immelmann turns and some other convolutions that made me feel alternately like a balloon and meat pâté, while the sky appeared to change from blue to dark gray and back to blue again.

While I teased my fears on this expensive military roller coaster, a hundred and twenty American soldiers, many of them on litters, were bumping slowly toward liberation with some of the most harrowing stories of the Korean War. It was just as well that I had amused myself while it was possible, because in Korea the fun was almost over.

22

The last phases of the Korean War were covered largely by press conferences. There were press conferences almost every day at Panmunjom, where the armistice agreement was gradually nearing completion. There were press conferences near Munsan at the United Nations POW reception camp, which was dubbed "Freedom Village."

The camp consisted of a helicopter landing ground and some large tents in a bulldozed mud clearing about twice the size of a football field. Two adjacent tents were allocated to the press. A press conference, along with delousing, a medical examination and a lecture from security officers, was part of most prisoners' return to freedom. They weren't compelled, but they were encouraged, to submit to questioning.

One by one, the men sat fidgeting or lay on stretchers at the focal point of dazzling floodlights and flash bulbs. Microphones were thrust close to their faces to record their words for radio, television, and newsreels. Correspondents asked questions gently and sympathetically, or with the sharp skepticism of prosecuting attorneys. Confused replies uttered hesitantly by teen-age illiterates whose minds had been muddled by Chinese political indoctrination were solemnly recorded on film and tape and in notebooks. The day the first prisoners returned, U.N. correspondents cabled approximately 250,000 words from Freedom Village, including many words expressing ideas that the ex-prisoners would almost certainly repudiate or forget after a short time back in the land of hamburgers and milk shakes and automobiles with white-wall tires.

There were some grim accounts of the first days of captivity just after China's sudden intervention during the first winter of the war. North Koreans marched American prisoners to camps near the Yalu in severe cold. There was no proper medical care for the wounded. One man told of having a gangrenous foot slowly cut off with a hacksaw, without anaesthetic. A fellow prisoner gave him the only available comforter—a stick to bite when the pain got bad.

But the most important and most interesting of the ex-prisoners' reports of their captivity were those on Chinese methods of "brainwashing" and its effects. After a short time I was convinced that the Chinese had been mostly unsuccessful, partly because of the mentalities of some of the men they had been trying to seduce. Physical attrition and degradation, threats and bribes, insults and flattery had induced some prisoners to broadcast and write letters in favor of ending the war; some others had at least ostensibly accepted Chinese charges that the United States was waging germ warfare against North Korea (of course there had been no opportunity for the prisoners to hear the American rebuttal of the charges); but the dialectics of Mao's brand of Marxism obviously had not been understood, much less retained, by the majority of the captive GI's, some of whom seemed to have more in common with Li'l Abner than with the sophisticated psychopaths and neurotics who are so prevalent among America's confirmed Communists.

After the exchanges of the sick and wounded prisoners, the war anticlimactically dragged on. President Rhee was determined to keep it going. He was convinced, not altogether without reason, that the only certain way to reunite his country was by force. The majority of the United Nations, on the other hand, considered that their work was finished when they had forced the invading North Koreans and their Chinese allies back to their side of the 38th parallel; reunification and elections were to be arranged by some future peace conference.

Meanwhile, the Chinese in the field were maintaining considerable military pressure on the U.N. line to help the Chinese at the bargaining table. The most formidable enemy attack of the last two years of the war was launched against the South Koreans, on the central front, less than two weeks before Armistice Day. It seemed as though the Chinese were trying to convince President Rhee that it would be folly for South Korea alone to attempt to continue the war.

Four ROK divisions were badly battered by Chinese artillery and Chinese infantrymen, who swarmed southward with the suicidal, inexorable determination of ants. I waded about in the mud (it was raining hard) with harassed United Nations liaison officers while South Korean soldiers fought hard but fell back. At dusk, as the fighting continued, and "the situation," as briefing officers used to say during retreats, remained "fluid," I organized my own withdrawal. An Army liaison plane managed to take off from a mud strip in a torrential downpour. We landed on Seoul Racetrack.

In the press billets, I got a Korean boy to scrape my boots. I had a shower and a shave. I put on a fresh uniform. I ate a hot dinner. Michael Rougier, who had been photographing the ROK's prize unit, the Capitol Division, taking a fearful beating, came into my room and asked: "Going to the fashion show?"

There was a carnival atmosphere in "Carnegie Hall," a new American-style Seoul night club. Miss Norah Noh, a South Korean *couturière* who had learned her business during a one-year sojourn in Los Angeles, had picked that night to present South Korea's first "Western" fashion show.

Tommy's Combo, a wild Korean jazz band, played "Sing, Sing, Sing," an old Goodman band arrangement featuring drums, while grotesquely painted Korean girls modeled black-market dresses in exaggerated Conover Girl attitudes, and Miss Noh tirelessly raised her thinly penciled left eyebrow in the *femme fatale* manner of silent movie vamps, as she pointed out the attractions of her latest designs.

"I can see the most fashionable colors in Korea next season are going to be recognition-panel yellow, foxhole brown, outpost green, bazooka gray and Nam Il red," Rougier commented sardonically.

The climax of the show was the antithesis of Korea's modest national dress: a young woman strutted around the dance floor wearing a red chimney pot hat trimmed with feathers, an off-the-shoulder white muslin blouse, and a multicolored transparent silk skirt. She sang a song that sounded like a mixture of "Arirang" and "Come on-a My House."

"This has been a hell of a day," Rougier said. "I can hardly wait to tell my grandchildren about the things I've seen—an all-out attack and an all-out surrealist nightmare."

At Panmunjom on July 27, 1953, the morning the Armistice was signed, I kept telling myself that I was witnessing history being made; however, like most other Westerners there, military and civilian alike, I failed to generate any feelings of great enthusiasm. There had been so many alternating days of wistful hope and listless anxiety that most people in Korea seemed to have lost the capacity for strong emotion, even on the last day of the war. There was no triumph on either side of the Communist-built, U.N.-lighted "Pagoda of Peace," which one American correspondent called, more aptly, "Compromise Castle." The unprofitable nature of modern warfare was never more clearly demonstrated.

The last hour of the war was the longest. I spent it with some Marines in a bunker on the forward slope of the main line of resistance. We counted the minutes. The cease-fire was due at 10 P.M. American and Chinese artillery had been particularly active all day. It was suggested that both sides wanted to reduce the weight of the ammunition they would have to carry when they pulled back from the demarcation zone. While the aimless explosions continued, everyone was extra careful not to get killed.

"I'd never forgive myself if I got killed the last day," Rougier said. He was planning to work continuously for the next forty-eight hours. We were sharing a helicopter and a bottle of benzedrine tablets that he had been able to get from the Marine Corps.

A Marine lieutenant counted off the last ten seconds of the war.

At zero, a corporal celebrating his twentieth birthday had the honor of firing a white signal flare to mark the end of hostilities at that part of the front.

The occasion was celebrated with lukewarm orange pop, "with artificial flavoring and coloring added."

Early the following morning, the helicopter landed Rougier and me in no man's land beside a steep hill called Boulder City. We climbed the hill on foot. The ground was thickly strewn with American and Chinese grenades, mortar shells, mines, artillery shells and shell fragments, burp-gun clips, and belts of machine-gun ammunition, some supposedly dud and some believed to be alive.

This was the point at which Americans and Chinese had most closely confronted each other at the end of the fighting. The opposing positions were actually connected by deep communication trenches. Americans and Chinese were often no more than 25 yards apart; sometimes they intruded into each other's positions and fought hand to hand.

The day before the cease fire they had been trying to kill each other. Now they were in each other's trenches retrieving their own dead.

The weather was hot. There was a heavy, sweet smell like the smell of rotten lilies. There was a buzz of flies. Bodies that had been unrecoverable during the past few days had swollen and blackened and putrified in the sunshine. Some, like inflated rubber dummies, had split the rotting cloth of their battle dress. Looking from the Americans to the Chinese and back again, one noticed that in death they were beginning to look alike.

Brigadier General J. C. Burger, second in command of the First Marines, visited Boulder City while Rougier and I were still there.

"The aftermath of war," the general said. "There's never been anything quite like this before. And I don't think we'll ever see anything like it again."

Silently, steadily, the stretcher-bearers walked back and forth.

At a souvenir stall at ground zero of the atomic bomb that devastated Hiroshima in August, 1945, K. Kikkawa, a member of an association called "The Atomic Bomb Casualty Sufferers" pulled off his shirt with hands like claws and reproachfully showed me the shiny pink and brown lumps of keloid scar tissue all over his back.

He offered me a smooth glass fragment that he said had been fused by the awful heat of atomic radiation. I gave him 100 yen (28 cents) for it. Afterward, I noticed that the glass had been part of a Coca Cola bottle. He was exacting his retribution in small installments.

At Tokyo University, Dr. Horotake Kakehi, a Japanese physicist, told me enthusiastically of the progress that Japan was making in nuclear research.

"We are still far behind you," he said. "But—who knows?—perhaps, one day. . . ."

On my return to the United States, I became preoccupied with the probable nature of World War III. My apprehensiveness was increased by an assignment to write a series of articles on Strategic Air Command, USAF. After a few months with my family in Baltimore, I flew to SAC headquarters, at Offutt Air Force Base, just outside Omaha, Nebraska, a city renowned for its beefsteak.

"Good meat begins with good grazing," a restaurateur pointed out. "But one of the most important factors is hanging it. None of this premature freezing. You've got to hang meat until the tissues begin to break down—this is for tenderness—and the whole carcass ripens—this is for flavor.

"What's the matter, mister? You're not feeling well?"

One of General Curtis E. LeMay's aides assured me that the bomb that was dropped on Hiroshima was now regarded as kids' stuff.

"If the explosive force of one ton of TNT were represented by a one-inch cube, the average load of a World War II bomber would be represented by a column four inches high," he said.

"The Hiroshima bomb would be represented by a column 1,666 *feet* high, three times as tall as the Washington Monument, and the thermonuclear superbomb would be represented by a column 63 *miles* high!

"With bombs of such cataclysmic potential and the means to deliver them," the general's aide recited, "the furies of war could be compressed into a very short period. Think what it would be like: Your whole city would be in flames. Casualties would be in the hundreds of thousands. The immediate need for plasma in one city would exceed the total amount used in the whole Korean War. You might be able to pull a few people out of the rubble. But don't forget that the fire department would have been destroyed by the same bomb, and the police department, and the ambulances, and the hospitals. And of course you couldn't expect any help from the next metropolis; they would have been hit too. . . ."

I flew down to Carswell Air Force Base, at Fort Worth, Texas. Major F. E. Bachmann, Jr. and fourteen other men took me up for a training flight in a B-36. From the height at which we were flying, the target, a football stadium, looked like a small bone curtain ring.

"That's Dallas?" I asked the pilot.

"That *was* Dallas," he replied with a boyish smile, as the vast plane banked and headed away at 400 miles an hour for the Gulf of Mexico.

I spent a lot of time brooding about Mr. Kikkawa, Dr. Kakehi, my family, General LeMay, Major Bachmann, and the politicians, the scientists, the military men, and the rest of the people all over the world, East and West, and the future that was being prepared.

It was a relief to turn my attention to a more immediate, comparatively cosy crisis, the struggle for domination of the Republic of Guatemala.

23

On my return from the Far East to the United States I had written to all the Latin American embassies in Washington to get on their information mailing lists. Most of them sent me brochures intended to attract tourists; but one country inundated me with newsletters and political pamphlets. This was Guatemala, whose quasi-Communist government complained that a plot to overthrow it was being organized with United States encouragement and support. The 1954 revolution against the régime of President Jacobo Arbenz Guzman was well advertised beforehand.

In May, 1954, the Swedish cargo ship *Alfhelm* sailed from Poland with a cargo of Czechoslovakian arms. The shipment, which was believed to be worth about $10,000,000, was originally cleared for Dakar. But the *Alfhelm* delivered the arms to Puerto Barrios, the Caribbean port of Guatemala. Later that month, after the State Department in Washington had called the delivery "a grave development," Dorsey, the managing editor, agreed that it might be interesting to see what was going on down there. I hadn't been to Central

America before and I spoke no Spanish, but I knew how to spell the name of the country and where it was on the map, and he sent me. Very few other managing editors became sufficiently interested to assign reporters to Guatemala until the airlines had stopped flying there, the frontiers were closed, and it was almost impossible to get in.

This was to be my first revolution. I went to the State Department for a briefing. A man in a small office closed the door and sat down at the Central American desk and opened, presumably, the Guatemalan drawer, and brought out a creased Guatemalan Esso map.

"May I see?" I asked, moving the map toward my side of the desk.

"I'm sorry," he said anxiously, seizing the map by one corner. "I can't let you have it. It's the only one I have. But if you like I'll try to get you one."

When he telephoned, however, the State Department's neighborhood Esso gas station was closed.

"Frankly, I'm stymied," he said with a worn Ivy-League smile that was half a frown. "Still, I can give you the names of the political parties, if that would help."

Eventually I got an Esso map from the United Fruit Company in Guatemala City. After the revolution I learned that leaders of both sides had been using Esso maps in their conduct of the brief military campaign.

In Baltimore, I went to Eddie Jacobs and asked for some suits made of miracle-fabric, suitable for a revolution.

"Bulletproof, you mean?" he said.

"No, washable."

I got two washable suits and a white dinner jacket on my expense account.

On the way southward I read a guidebook that had been supplied by the Guatemalan embassy: "Guatemala (From Where the Rainbow Takes Its Colors)." Guatemala, the book said, and the book was right, is "The Land of Eternal Spring . . . ancient, historical, colorful, picturesque, modern." It was heaven on earth, for a while: the sweet, wooden chimes of marimbas in flower-scented patios kept one from hearing the groans of political prisoners in the basement of the headquarters of the Guardia Civil.

Gerry Robichaud, of the Chicago *Sun-Times*, had arrived in Guatemala City two days ahead of me and was a model assimilator of local color. A dark, swarthy man, he was growing a wild black moustache which he hoped would look authentically Latin in time for the revolution. He was already properly dressed, in a brown suit and a black tie.

"Don't drink in the hotel bar," he said. "The *cantinero*—the bartender—speaks English. Come across the street with me. I'm learning Spanish. This is better than Berlitz.

"Hey, Joe," he said, "una cerveza Bohémia, por favor, and para this señor here, uno martini, muy seco." Robichaud turned to me in triumph. "All in two days," he said. "But don't feel bad. You'll catch on.

"Hey, Joe," he said, proudly displaying more of his erudition, "bocitas." Bocitas proved to be canapés, strips of fatty ham and bean paste, rather like peanut butter, on crackers. "And I've discovered a new drink, made of pineapple juice, lime, coffee essence, and white rum. It's great."

"How about sources?" I asked. "Have you found anyone helpful?"

"This bartender knows everything about everything," Robichaud assured me. "The revolution's due the third week of the month. That gives us plenty of time to look around. I've lined up most of the cabinet for interviews. I'm doing Toriello, the foreign minister, tomorrow. You can come along, if you want to. And I've found a good Spanish restaurant—chicken and shrimp and rice, and not too greasy. I've just about got this town figured out."

Antigua Guatemala, the sixteenth century Spanish colonial capital, was badly damaged by earthquake and flood in the eighteenth century. The eruption was interpreted as a Providential hint to the survivors to move away. Guatemala City was established soon afterward, about a mile above sea level. It, too, was laid waste by earthquakes, in 1917 and 1918; but omens of this sort are disregarded in the present century, and the city was largely rebuilt. Most of it today is modern; some of it is vaguely traditional. It is not a great architectural achievement, but an almost perfect climate makes one feel so well that the minor beauties of the capital are greatly enhanced.

The Penitentiary and Police Headquarters are forts with crenelated battlements, but they don't look severe or even serious: the Penitentiary is pale green and Police Headquarters is pale pink. There are orange-tiled white villas in tropical gardens.

The population of Guatemala City is more than 300,000, about a tenth of the national population. The capital is by far the most important city of the Republic, and the Parque Central, a large plaza, is the heart of the nation. The buildings lining the four sides of the square (the National Palace, the barracks, the Cathedral, and offices and shops) represent the four competing powers: the Government, the Army, the Church, and Commerce. One can find a few chips caused by bullets in the stucco. In this square the revolutions begin and end. What happens in the provinces is incidental.

The Pan-American Hotel, only a block from the commercial side of the plaza and only a few minutes' walk from a cable office, is the hotel in which most correspondents stay while covering Guatemalan revolutions. Not knowing the layout of the city when I arrived, I stayed first at the Palace Hotel, which is slightly nearer the Government Tourist Bureau. I wanted to see some of the rest of the country before it was too late.

When I was ushered into the private office of Guillermo Palmieri, the director of the Tourist Bureau, he was sitting at his desk loading a pearl-handled .38 revolver. He looked up and smiled a Caesar Romero smile. Palmieri had the high sheen of a Latin lover: his black hair, his dark eyes, his white teeth, and his black silk sport shirt gleamed.

"Ah!" he exclaimed with cordiality that seemed only partly sarcastic. "The great Baltimore *Sun!* An editor of yours was down here a few months ago."

"Yes," I said.

"I flew him in my own plane. We landed in the dry bed of a river delta. He was very frightened. He is a polite man, but I could notice that he was unhappy. His name is Mr. Ives. Is he a Fascist?"

"No, not a Fascist," I said.

"But he doesn't believe in sharing with the people," Palmieri insisted.

"He believes in American constitutional law and free enterprise," I said.

"You mean United States constitutional law, I suppose. He believes in a lot of crap," Palmieri said with a charming smile, speaking in the patient voice of a kindergarten teacher trying to convey to a backward child a simple, important truth. "But he is a very nice, polite gentleman. We had many fine arguments. If you believe in something you must be prepared to defend it—do you not agree?" I did not want to argue, especially since Palmieri had snapped into place the loaded cylinder of the revolver and was now shutting first one eye, then the other, as he looked thoughtfully across the sights at various objects in the room.

"Yes, I agree to that," I said. "But what I really came here for—"

"You know, it is very interesting," Palmieri said smoothly, as he pointed his revolver at a bird on a pictorial wall map of Guatemala. "I look with one eye and see that the bird is in the sights; I look with the other eye and the bird is no longer in the sights: the aim changes according to the point of view. Do you agree?"

"That sounds plausible," I acknowledged. "I was wondering, though—"

"Ah!" Palmieri shouted, abruptly leaning forward in his swivel chair and slapping his desk with his free hand. "Then what is true for one eye may not be true for another! There is no absolute truth. I was taught by Jesuits," Palmieri said. "They are very clever men, very clever. I am a Catholic"—he pulled at a fine gold chain around his neck—"but I tell you that sometimes their religion is not the same as my religion." His conversational tactics had silenced me. I waited. I did not have to wait long.

"You know what kind of bird that is?" Palmieri demanded.

"A parrot of some kind?"

"It is a quetzal," Palmieri said with somber pride. "It is a very independent bird. If you put it in a cage, it will not eat; it will die. This is the national emblem of Guatemala. But does the United Fruit Company remember that?"

"Really," I began again, "all I want—"

"Can you use a gun?" Palmieri asked. "Could you shoot the head of that little quetzel with the first shot?"

"I'd rather not try," I said.

"Ah!" Palmieri said. "I am glad. Because if you kill the quetzal, I will kill you. Please write *that* to your Baltimore *Sun* and to all the

North American people. Why does Mr. Dulles attack Guatemala? How can we threaten your Panama Canal? Do you like Mr. Dulles?"

"I do not like him or dislike him," I replied untruthfully. "He is the United States Secretary of State. I am a reporter."

"I have been to the United States," Palmieri said. "And also I have stood beside Jacobo Arbenz Guzman while guns were firing. He is the President of Guatemala, and I am a Guatemalan."

"And the director of the National Tourist Bureau," I reminded him. He accepted the rebuke with a nod and a smile.

"You want to see Antigua and Lake Atitlán and Chichicastenango?" Palmieri said. "Of course—they are the most beautiful places in the world. I will take you myself—tomorrow morning. I will show you the wicked Communists cultivating their fields and plotting to blow up Miami Beach."

"I don't want you to take me anywhere," I said. "I just want some information."

"Information! I'll give you information! I insist on taking you. To tell the truth, I am conducting this tour anyway. You are not the only journalist who has thought of it. There are two or three others who have already applied. We will leave at about 11:30—in time to get to Antigua for cocktails before lunch. There will be much conversation."

He was an offensive man. But I found it impossible to dislike him.

"I'll pick you up at your hotel," he said.

"I'm at the Palace."

"I know," he said.

"About how much money will I need?"

Palmieri laughed.

"Now you are joking," he said. "You, yourself, have pointed out that I am the director of the National Tourist Bureau. . . . I think I like you, but Mr. Ives argues better."

"We are taking with us a young woman from Berkeley, California," Palmieri said the next morning. "She is not a journalist and she is not pretty, but she has very splendid breasts. She told me she is interested in agrarian reform and public hygiene. I have met other idealistic, cultured North American ladies. With their mouths they

138

ask questions about the Mayan pyramids at Zaculeu; but with their eyes—even the dried-up old schoolteachers with the faces of horses —they all ask for only one thing. I will explain agrarian reform and public hygiene to the young woman from Berkeley, California. Then I will show her the moonlight on Lake Atitlán."

I asked him why he was telling me his plans for her.

"As long as I know that you know what I am thinking," he explained, "it will add a certain spice to the political discussions during the drive," he said. "The two other journalists will be taken by my assistant in the second car."

Palmieri drove like a demon. Miss F——— sat beside him, and I sat in the back. She had yellow hair, brushed up, surmounted by a circular ropelike plait. She wore horn-rimmed spectacles and no make-up. Her complexion was fair. She was dressed in folksy Guatemalan clothes, a white blouse and a multicolored coarse woolen skirt. She looked as earnestly, wholesomely romantic as a Scandinavian cello player.

She asked him scores of questions about crop rotation and DDT spraying. He answered them with hot, smoldering glances, gazing at her as languidly as was possible at high speeds on a road that wound between a sheer cliff and a sheer precipice.

At an open space the car slithered to a halt and Palmieri turned to me and grinned and said: "Let me show you some of my gun collection." We got out and he opened the trunk of the car. It was an arsenal. There were automatics and rifles and a submachine gun and several grenades.

"We shall have a contest, you and I," he told me. I could see why I wasn't driving in the other car. I was to be his tame rival.

Palmieri placed a Kodak film package on a boulder and led me about a hundred feet from it.

"Go on and shoot it," he said, "like this." He raised his revolver like an accusative finger and shot. There was a tiny eruption of stone-dust close to the yellow cardboard of the improvised target. He handed me the revolver and smiled at Miss F———, whose face was expressionless. It was my turn. Suddenly I wanted very much to hit the target. I lifted the revolver in the prescribed training-range manner, until my arm was fully outstretched. My hand trembled. I aimed carefully and gradually squeezed the trigger.

When my eyes blinked open the film container was no longer on the boulder. Palmieri and I looked toward the woman. She was looking at her watch.

"But of course anybody can shoot straight if he takes enough time," Palmieri quickly commented. "When fighting in the streets the important factor is speed. Look. Imagine that the boulder is a man." He snatched the revolver from me and walked rapidly away from the boulder. "I hear a suspicious noise!" he shouted—"immediately I turn and fire—" there were four rapid bangs, four hits. "That's the way to do it," he said. "The man is dead; I am alive."

The woman said nothing.

"Good grouping," I said uneasily.

"All right," Palmieri said grimly. "Let's go."

That night we stayed in an attractive hotel near Lake Atitlán. Palmieri and the young woman dined by themselves and left the building soon after dinner.

The next morning his car was gone.

I was finishing breakfast, while the two other correspondents and Palmieri's assistant were checking out of their rooms, when the young woman came into the dining room.

"May I join you for a cup of coffee?" she asked. "I'd like to tell you what happened last night. I know what you must think. Mr. Palmieri took me for a walk. We went to the beach. It was beautiful."

I sat sipping my coffee and applying what Max Beerbohm once called, I think, "the spur of silence."

"Well, yes, he made a pass at me," she continued in a surprisingly matter-of-fact tone of voice. "I spoke a bit sharply to him. And— guess what! It was worse than when you hit that Kodak box at point-blank range this afternoon, after he'd missed the damn thing."

"What did he do?" I asked.

"He burst right out crying and ran away."

24

Colonel Carlos Castillo Armas, who had tunneled out of the Guatemala City penitentiary a couple of years before, was in the neighboring republic of Honduras, waging a war of nerves against the Arbenz régime. The Honduran Government was allowing him to operate a C-47 from a base in their country. He sent it over Guatemala to drop leaflets, and, some said, arms.

"Fight for God, country, liberty, work, truth, justice!" one of the leaflets exhorted the people of Guatemala. "Fight against Communist atheism, Communist oppression, Communist poverty, Communist lies, Communist police! Fight with your brother patriots—fight with Castillo Armas!"

A rebel radio station, a mobile transmitter, was heard in the Guatemalan capital.

"Arbenz, your days are numbered," it warned. "Your tomb is prepared and the buzzards are flying around it, awaiting you and your band of assassins."

The Minister of the Interior announced that police had arrested revolutionary plotters and seized weapons and explosives. He said that expatriate Guatemalans were receiving foreign aid to organize their campaign against the Guatemalan Government. Guatemalans were said to be hoarding food and gasoline. Prices were going up. Metal shutters were locked over the windows of stores.

There were more arrests. Some anti-Communists gained asylum in sympathetic foreign embassies. One of the fugitives was the editor of the most outspoken anti-Government newspaper, *El Espectador*, J. A. P. Palmieri, the Tourist Bureau director's older brother.

There were rumors of police brutalities.

There were rumors that the Arbenz government was distributing Czechoslovakian machine guns among the Indians.

"I'd rather be machine-gunned than sliced up with a machete," said a former mayor of Guatemala City at the bar of the Palace Hotel. "But after the next drink I shall return to my plantation. I will make it a fort. Mine will be the Dien Bien Phu of the coffee *fincas*."

In the market town of Chichicastenango, where all sorts of goods, from scratchy old Charleston records to coffins, were for sale, the *Maxenos* were locally regarded as so gentle and honest that the hotel doors were constructed without locks. In San Antonio Palopo, a small, pre-Colombian village, I had seen Cakchiquel men in skirts and turbans, sitting in the shade, smoking and knitting. It was difficult to imagine Guatemalan Indians engaging in violence with weapons of any kind. But the former mayor assured me that an Indian would cut off your arm as soon as look at you.

On June 8, the government announced the suspension of civil liberties. Police could now enter homes without warrants, legally. *Habeas corpus* writs were no longer valid. Public meetings were forbidden. Censorship was imposed on local and outgoing news articles. The rebel radio said that Castillo would strike soon.

A taxi driver was more precise: "The revolution will begin in ten days," he said. The taxi driver was right.

The Austrian proprietor of La Casita, which the government guidebook characterized as "the most aristocratic of all tearooms and restaurants" of Guatemala City, wrung his hands anxiously.

"Aie!" he wailed. "Comes now more heartache! My dears, I can tell you—here no pleasure is."

By the time Guatemala's frontiers closed for the duration of the emergency, about a dozen foreign correspondents were installed in Guatemala City. Others had joined Castillo Armas in Honduras. One of the last American newspapermen to arrive in the capital was Fred Sparks, then of N.E.A.

I saw him on arrival, hesitating fastidiously in the main doorway of the Pan-American Hotel, into which, by then, most of us had moved. Sparks was a correspondent's correspondent, a classic journalistic type, unchanged but for minutiae since I had last seen him in Seoul: his soft hat was on the back of his head, the last few millimeters of a cigarette hung attached to his lower lip, his trench coat was open, and he was almost entirely unencumbered, except by a few German and Japanese cameras.

Sparks has a phenomenally flexible nose and a curiously deliberate way of twitching its tip rapidly from side to side, as though testing the atmosphere, before speaking. He twitched a bit at this moment of reunion, inclined his head forward, peered over his spectacles, and, with something of W. C. Fields's querulousness in his tone of voice, inquired: "Where, may I ask, are the barricades? Where are the babies skewered on bayonets? Where's the cable office? And where's the bar? I have a deadline, you know."

Later, as we walked across the central plaza, he said that he was, frankly, rather taken aback by the paucity of evidence of national turmoil. It was showing remarkably little in the streets.

"But let's not knock the story," he added hastily. "It's getting a very nice play in the States. Wonderful stuff, wonderful stuff. . . ."

One of his fundamental rules, he went on, was to file immediately on arrival at a trouble spot, before risking the confusion of conflicting impressions; it was lucky he had got his story off before seeing the empty streets. Again there was that telltale twitching, a slight hint of madness in the roll of the eyes.

"These are parlous times," he declaimed in a manner suitable for broadcasting. He had a working arrangement with the National Broadcasting Corporation, which was to pay him $50 for every 90-second telephone call on the revolution. "Mr. and Mrs. America:

there's a dark cloud no bigger than a man's hand over the National Palace tonight—or has somebody already said that?

"But where's my kit?" he demanded, turning savagely on a small, barefoot shoeshine boy. "How can I win a Nobel Prize without my Hermes? This is an outrage! Take me to Pan-American Airways! Take me to President Arbenz! What a way to run a crisis! This is going to mean his job. . . ."

Sparks doesn't settle down in a strange country, but after he has been around for a while the country gradually adapts itself. Robichaud was still conducting seminars over the martinis and *bocitas*, but Sparks scorned such concessions to the natives.

"They're Reds aren't they?" he said. "The hell with them."

When the use of Spanish words was unavoidable, he mangled them with careless hauteur or with the malicious inaccuracy of Churchill growling "Nazzy" for Nazi. While Sparks is actually a sound and industrious reporter, he operates in disguise, so to speak. He has an encyclopaedic knowledge of journalistic clichés and tricks which he manifests almost incessantly in conversation, like a living parody of the code of Pulitzer rendered into a script by S. J. Perelman.

Over coffee and pastries, for example, after two of his colleagues had just exchanged their day's collection of unconfirmed and unconfirmable reports from the Honduran border, Sparks looked furtively over one shoulder and then the other, put the back of one hand beside his mouth, and said: "I'm putting machine guns in the church steeple at Puerto Barrios in my dispatch tonight, men. In these revolutions they always put machine guns in the church steeples. Just a friendly tip. You guys are going to look pretty silly if you don't get those machine guns up there."

His satirical manner sometimes had a salutary effect on the rest of us, including more than one who were somewhat inclined to introduce added melodrama into a situation that was already, goodness knew, quite cloak-and-daggerish enough.

Censorship was becoming a major problem. Carlos Gonzalez Orellana, the chief censor and one of the known Communists in the government, was bitterly anti-American, and seemed to be making conditions as difficult as possible. In Korea, United Nations censorship, administered by the U.S. Army, had been occasionally irritating but usually logical and always impartial. In Guatemala I realized that I had been spoiled, for here I encountered the most capricious, arbitrary, and severe kind of restriction—censorship determined by political policies.

Our stories, with Spanish translations, were processed very slowly. The censors suspended operations during the long afternoon siesta and at night, and there were complaints from our editors.

The censors' alterations were supposed to be secret; and when friends at the cable office secretly showed them to us, we saw why we weren't supposed to know what was being done. Some of the censors were practicing what one might call "creative censorship," actually changing the meanings of stories by deletions and even, in extreme cases, by additions.

I went to the chief censor's office and complained. He was a plump man with a round, pale yellow face that looked as though it never had to be shaved, and bifocals with lenses as thick as ice cubes through which he blinked sadly as he listened to my diatribe. When I had finished he sighed.

"The trouble is that we don't like what you write," he said. "You write too many lies. You should go back and try to do better." Back to Macao, I thought.

When I returned to the hotel, some other correspondents were already discussing the vicissitudes of censorship.

"I bet a correspondent for *Pravda* wouldn't be handicapped this way," I said. This notion gave me an idea which, at the time, seemed to be a good one. "It would be interesting to see how the censors would handle a party-line message, wouldn't it? Wouldn't their treatment of it demonstrate to the world just where their sympathies lie?"

Paul Kennedy of the New York *Times*, Tom Gerber of the Boston *Traveler*, and Jack Rutledge of the Associated Press, were among the people who helped me to refine the scheme. Then I concocted what I thought was an obvious parody of a Soviet article on the situation in Guatemala. I chastised "the running dogs of reaction" and praised the government for having suspended civil liberties "to stabilize the nation at this time when decency and courage are being threatened by cynical and mercenary backsliding counterrevolutionary conspirators." My colleagues read it and agreed that if the censors approved it there could no longer be the slightest vestige of doubt about the true nature of the Arbenz régime.

The censor on duty in the cable office read the dispatch and took it himself on a motorcycle to censorship headquarters. A few minutes later he was back again and my copy was slapped on top of the pile, for immediate transmission. I felt that the experiment was already proving successful. Meanwhile, I had sent a brief service message, not subject to censorship, saying: "Counting on you to provide appropriate introduction to forthcoming article."

The late John E. Peurifoy, U.S. Ambassador to Guatemala, when the crisis had approached its climax had set up a daily confidential news briefing for American correspondents. The morning after my *Pravda*-style cable had been sent, the usual group gathered in his private office: the ambassador and his public affairs officer and we correspondents. Peurifoy, who was usually heartily cheerful, looked strangely withdrawn and grim.

"Before I begin the briefing this morning," he said, "I'm going to read aloud a cable that one of you sent yesterday. By the time I finish reading it I imagine that man will want to leave the embassy. And as far as I'm concerned he had better not come back again. . . ." Then he began to read my cable.

"No, not that!" I protested in the manner of the abused heroine of a Victorian melodrama. Peurifoy looked up puzzled as Kennedy and Rutledge also raised their voices to halt the reading. There were hurried explanations. The ambassador's face relaxed until it positively shone with relief.

"Well, you crazy son-of-a-bitch!" he addressed me affectionately after the others had left. "You had us worried there for a few hours. Why didn't you tell us what you were going to do? I thought we had a Commie in our midst."

Peurifoy told me that my office had applied urgently to the State Department, in Washington, to try to find out through the department's channels of communication whether I had been taken prisoner and was being forced to write seditious propaganda, or whether I had simply gone mad. I was notified that I was to stop

146

work until I was able to explain to my office the circumstances that had produced the story. Peurifoy allowed me to send a coded radio message to Washington and thence to Baltimore explaining the whole chain of events.

The explanation was satisfactory. The *Sun* ran a front-page story headed "Guatemalan Censorship: Not a Word Is Deleted from Fake 'Red' Cable."

The incident was closed. Peurifoy was particularly friendly after that, and after we both left Guatemala we kept in touch. We had lunch together in Baltimore shortly before he went to Bangkok as the U.S. ambassador to Thailand, and to his death in a sports car.

I have sometimes wondered what might have happened in the embassy in Guatemala if the New York *Times* and the Associated Press had not been in on the act. And since then I have never forgotten this basic rule of journalism: Do not write irony, unless you clearly label it "JOKE." Even the most absurd written words can look awfully serious at the receiving end of a teleprinter.

The whereabouts and state of health of President Arbenz were unknown. He had been assassinated, said the manager of the hotel. The president's opponents had placed him under house arrest, said the headwaiter. The president had fled the country with a suitcase full of dollars, the waiter said. After breakfast, Fred Sparks and I walked across the sunlit plaza to the National Palace to try to find out who was president.

The office of propaganda and information was too busy censoring news to disseminate any, so we called on Garcia Galvez, a smartly tailored, tidily moustachioed gentleman who looked very much like Adolph Menjou in one of his earlier, lighter roles. This was the chief protocol officer. He was charmingly uninformative. He smiled and nodded and agreed that it would be a very good idea for a foreign reporter to be shown President Arbenz sitting in his executive suite in order to prove that he was alive and well and active in office; but, sad to say, this proof was impossible to arrange at the moment; the president was at home, very busy, and not to be disturbed.

Foreign Minister Toriello, who had promised about a week be-

147

fore to see reporters, but who had postponed indefinitely all appointments with the press because of "sickness," was then seen striding vigorously into the palace. Señor Galvez said that he would relay our questions to the foreign minister. Half an hour later, the chief protocol officer returned to the waiting room and said:

"What a pity. The ladies have got him." I walked quickly to the doorway and looked out; indeed, the ladies did have him. Foreign Minister Toriello, wearing a dove-gray suit, heavy dark glasses, and a bright smile, was leaning elegantly against wrought-iron railings beside an ornamental pool in the patio, exchanging pleasantries with three women.

"One cannot compete with the ladies," Señor Galvez gratuitously observed, "but he answered all your questions. He said they were all *bolas*—rumors. I am sorry, gentlemen: nothing is true."

An information officer showed us a portfolio of new clippings from the radical press of France and Italy.

"The opinion of the world," he said. "You can read how other nations sympathize with us."

United States citizens, about 600 in the capital and 600 in the provinces, were advised to stay at home. Militiamen were stopping and searching automobiles.

Sparks and I took a taxi to the Mayan Golf Club. Sparks is a fervent believer in regular exercise as a means of clarifying the brain. The taxi driver said:

"It will be tonight."

"What will?" Sparks asked.

"The revolution, sir."

"Oh, *that*," Sparks said. "You like?"

"Very good, sir."

"Number one," Sparks agreed, relapsing absentmindedly into Oriental pidgin.

I lay beside the pool while Sparks earnestly plodded back and forth. When he had arrived in the country his thin, sinewy legs had looked like celery; now they were as red as rhubarb.

"Look at me, look at me," he said. "I'm a running dog of reaction. Let's swim. I'll watch you drive some golf balls over the wall

148

into the squatters' shacks. We'll have a couple of daiquiris and a steak or two. Then it'll be time for the revolution. O.K.?"

The afternoon passed in the usual sequence of siesta, expanding cumulus cloud, and torrential downpour. More rumors were served with coffee and pastries at 4 P.M.

"Tonight," the waiter confided. "The radio has said so."

The sonorous, hollow bonging of the cathedral bells rolled across the plaza, and somewhere in the distance sounded the mad, anachronistic crowing of a cock.

The cabinet held a five-hour emergency session.

Darkness fell.

At 10:42 P.M., a throbbing drone was heard. A two-motored plane passed slowly over the capital.

The proprietor of La Casita turned off the recorded marimba music and announced that his place was closing.

At 10:44, all the lights went out.

Outside the San Carlos Hotel, a woman in curlers and a dressing gown asked pedestrians what was happening. Cars and motorcycles headed for the suburbs. The plaza was as empty and sinister as a painting by Chirico. The cathedral towers were silhouetted against moonlit clouds like curdled milk. Two policemen in baggy pale-blue uniforms leaned against a stuccoed wall with their carbines held loosely at their sides.

Quiet.

The Guardia Civil headquarters was dark. The penitentiary was dark. The airport was dark. Sentries patrolled the barbed-wire perimeter fence. The black barrel of an automatic rifle moved out from a dark horizontal slit in a concrete pillbox.

Just as the taxi slowly left the airport road the lights went on again.

"Perhaps everything's all right?" I suggested.

"No," the driver assured me, "nothing is all right."

The next morning Foreign Minister Toriello announced that the country had been bombed and that an army of mercenaries was about to cross the border from Honduras.

"The battle for Guatemala has begun," he said.

149

25

A popular demonstration of loyalty to President Arbenz was scheduled to take place near the Guatemala City railroad terminus on the first morning of the revolution.

All night, dilapidated buses loaded with peasants had been converging on the station from outlying rural districts. Barefooted laborers in open shirts and ragged straw hats were lying in the shade trying to sleep until the great rally was due to begin.

Accompanied by Gerber, of the *Traveler*, I was making movies of the torpid scene. I took some shots of the buses' exotic name plates, of wall posters exhorting the people to arise and smash the foreign invasion, and some of the people curled up in fetal positions on the sidewalk. I was photographing a local union organizer handing out Mexican Communist literature to Guatemalan illiterates (a nice close-up of an ancient plantation worker studying a pamphlet upside down), and I heard a sudden, shrill, angry voice quite close, just off-camera, shouting: "Imperialista! Imperialista!"

I looked away from the camera to see a small man in a wrinkled brown suit, his face tense with rage, his bony fist shaking above his head.

"Imperialista!" he shouted. He was looking at me with concentrated passionate hatred.

"Who, me?" I said, pointing to my own chest and looking around.

"Yanqui!" he shouted. I could have kicked myself for wearing a seersucker suit. Robichaud had been so right to assume protective local coloring.

"Frutero!"

This last epithet was the name that had been given to the men of the United Fruit Company. I had little sympathy with the company, whose exploitation of Guatemala was largely to blame, in my opinion, for Communist infiltration of the agricultural and railway workers' unions, and, indeed, for the general deterioration of American prestige throughout the Republic.

"No frutero—periodista," I pointed out, not that American newspapermen were likely to be particularly popular at the moment. "Stringing for the London Daily Mail," I added. "Londres." I couldn't think of the Spanish word for "stringer." Newly awakened Indians were gathering around us. Their expressions ranged from stupidity, to curiosity, to irritation.

"Imperialistas!" the little Guatemalan shouted.

"Imperialistas!" repeated one of the less unintelligent apprentice demonstrators.

"Hey, it's plural now," Gerber complained to me. "You and your goddamn camera."

As the crowd enlarged with increasing animation, and the chanting loudened, we started backing away, not very casually, toward our taxi. The rabble rouser and his obedient rabble followed. When we got into the taxi and rolled up the windows, I noticed that we were surrounded. The leader shouted some angry instructions in Spanish.

"Let's go," I told our driver. "Hotel. O.K.?"

"Not O.K.," said the driver, who looked as frightened as I was beginning to feel. "This man is Victor Manuel Gutierrez. Top Communista. Very bad man."

"But if you just drive away . . . ?"

"No," the driver said, sadly shaking his head. "I drive, they kill me." He drew a fingernail across his throat.

"They'll probably kill us anyway," Gerber said. "Boy—what a story! The first American casualties!"

"Maybe we could ask Gutierrez to let us file our last words," I suggested with ponderous sarcasm. "An exclusive."

A policeman holding a revolver was opening the door of the taxi and gesturing for us to get out. It suddenly occurred to me that the life of a bank clerk would not be without a certain serene charm.

"All right, you wise guys," Gutierrez said. "We know what to do with people like you." For a schoolteacher, or a former schoolteacher, he was an uncouth person. He spewed out a turbulent stream of Spanish. It seemed uncomplimentary, even before he spat. The crowd shouted. It was shouting now as a unit. Then, puzzlingly, we were ordered back into the taxi.

It moved away from the crowd very slowly, followed by a gray police jeep. The jeep shepherded the taxi back to its customary stand in front of the hotel. I got out and walked as briskly as I dared toward the main entrance, but a policeman from the other jeep got there ahead of me. His revolver was in his holster, perhaps in deference to downtown sensibilities but he was holding a flexible truncheon with which he indicated that I was to turn around and get into his jeep. Gutierrez, who had unexpectedly appeared nearby, also pointed at the jeep. Gerber and I hesitated. There were several pedestrians watching. Surely, something could be done?

"I want to telephone my embassy!" I told Gutierrez in a loud voice. "Gerber wants to telephone the American Embassy too."

The policeman drew his revolver, and we stopped hesitating.

As we walked across the street toward the jeep, a man got out of an English Ford and said quietly, "Are you being taken in?" and I nodded my head and he went back to his car. This convenient witness was the Number Two man at the British Legation. He immediately called the United States Embassy. But at the time Gerber and I did not know who the man was or whether he could or would do anything to help us.

There were already three other policemen in the jeep, a driver and two men in the back with machine-pistols across their laps. The jeep was a weatherproof one: it had a small boxlike superstructure of plywood and canvas. I tried to climb into the back as one of the policemen was trying to climb out. Meanwhile, Gerber was close behind me, the fourth policeman was behind him, and Gutierrez was impatiently bringing up the rear.

A rather comic awkwardness occurred—that is to say, it might have been comic in other circumstances. At one point, the small cabin was full of writhing bodies trying to push past each other in opposite directions. At last, heated and ruffled, breathing hard, their caps disarranged, the police were able to readjust themselves. Now Gerber was between the two on the narrow back seat, I was perched sideways on the side of the Jeep between the rear and the front seats, and the driver and a policeman and Gutierrez were sitting very upright in front. We were all squeezed together tight and rigid.

"Are we under arrest?" I asked the back of Gutierrez's neck, which was shiny with sweat. He did not answer. The back of his neck looked extraordinarily hostile; for a neck it was unusually expressive. And his white shirt was dingy and frayed at the edge. I did not ask any more questions.

Each escorted by a pair of police, we followed Gutierrez up the broad steps of the pink fortress of the Guardia Civil. Since the battle for Guatemala had begun, the police had been militarized. There were open packing cases of new automatic weapons on the pretty tiled floor of the inner hall. Gutierrez left us standing in the hall under the supervision of a policeman with a submachine gun and swaggered into the office of the chief of police.

He didn't come out again.

After about twenty minutes, an Army officer came out. He was most courteous. He asked Gerber and me if we would kindly show some sort of identification. We showed our passports.

"You have a visa for Honduras," he said to me, more in sorrow than in anger.

"Yes," I admitted—he was looking right at it. "But I'm not go-

153

ing to leave Guatemala until the revolution has been . . . ended."
I couldn't have got out of the country even if I had wanted to, even
if I hadn't been under arrest.

"Hmmm," the officer said judiciously, as though weighing the
facts. "The Government of Honduras has not been sympathetic, you
know. But if you say that you do not intend to go there. . . ."

"I will stay in Guatemala until the end," I promised.

Clearly, he welcomed the chance to be magnanimous. He said
that we were to be released immediately.

"My camera," I said. "May I have my camera back, or a receipt
for it? Otherwise my office will be so cross with me."

"Camera?" the officer said. "Oh, yes—of course, of course. Now
that we know who you are, you shall receive it right away." So
Gutierrez didn't even get to keep the camera he had confiscated.

Although I couldn't say with certainty, it is my belief that
Gutierrez's highhanded manner and the call from the U.S. Embassy, combined with the Army's dissatisfaction with civilian Communist leaders and its anxieties about the situation in general had
resulted in a thoroughly unsatisfactory back-room interview for him.

If there's one thing that most Guatemalans really abhor, it is
discourtesy to the winning side.

26

Before the "battle for Guatemala" had actually got under way, censorship had become an increasingly serious handicap. It had been relatively easy to overcome as long as the airlines were still operating. Outward-bound passengers carried press messages and duly cabled or mailed them from the first airport-of-call outside Guatemala to our offices in the United States. Some correspondents referred to these cooperative passengers as "pigeons." Fred Sparks, who had arrived just in time to avail himself of this service, persuaded an excited American matron to secrete a dispatch in her bosom and assured her that she was helping to operate the most important airlift since Berlin.

But then, as the news became more sensational, the flying stopped, and the censorship of cables became far more stringent than it had been.

For two happy days I used the obvious alternative means of getting my copy out of the country. I went to Tropical Radio and simply telephoned my office. But other correspondents got the same idea. While the cable censors sat twiddling their thumbs, the single radio-telephone circuit from Guatemala to Miami was continuously busy. Foreign Minister Toriello complained that he had to wait hours to get through to his government's representatives in Washington.

Having checked on the outgoing calls, the government extended censorship to the telephone. Until the senior telephone censor came on duty, it seemed that our future chances of getting stories out of the country would be bad. But the chief telephone censor was a renegade British Honduran Negro who was short of cash. His name was Gerald Cattousse Fairweather.

He had been one of the organizers of the People's United Party, whose principal aim, then as now, was British Honduran secession from the British Commonwealth. He had emigrated to the adjacent republic of Guatemala to broadcast anti-British propaganda in English for listeners in Belize. Guatemala under Arbenz, as under previous and succeeding governments, claimed British Honduras as Guatemalan territory.

In Belize his surname was Fairweather. He dropped it in Guatemala, because he felt it was too English for his political beliefs. By June, 1954, he spoke fluent Spanish and was known as Señor Cattousse, and yet he persisted in a curious, illogical family pride. "My name is really Fairweather," he would say. "I'm no Guatemalan."

He was thirty-one years old, tall and slender, handsome and flashy. He had a head like an elongated coconut, with frizzy hair cut very short. His complexion was as light and smooth as *café au lait*. His eyes glittered and his teeth were big and even and white. He wore a pale blue suit with heavily padded shoulders, a long jacket and narrow trousers, and his shoes were long and narrow and pointed and two-toned, black and white.

His new duty was to stand beside the radio-telephone operator's switchboard, to wear earphones, to monitor long-distance conversations, and, if anything censorable were said about the military or political situation, to break the connection.

He was a vain man, and he loved to talk, especially about himself. Sparks and I each took turns distracting Cattousse while the other called the United States. The simple ruse seemed to work

156

satisfactorily, because Cattousse was eager to tell us the story of his life. But though he was vain, he was not blind or dumb.

After a day of unrestricted calls, including two to NBC for broadcasting, Cattousse said, in his mellifluous West Indian sing-song, "You know, I am being pretty nice to you and Mr. Sparks."

"What do you mean?" I asked.

"Well," he said, "you know, I have noticed how you chaps have been breaking through what you might call—ha, ha—'the Banana Curtain.' Mr. Luna, in the tourist office, has told me that you even flew down to San Salvador one afternoon—not for the scenery, I suppose."

"Luna said that?"

"Yes, he did. You know it's true, now, don't you, sir?"

"I went to see a doctor about my hay fever," I said.

"Yes, that's a good one. But it was very expensive, was it not? I mean, the fare there and back, the exit permits, the visa, the re-entry permit? Those American papers must have plenty of money."

I conceded that point.

"And now the planes are flying no longer, until the emergency is over. But the telephone has been working very nicely today, don't you think?"

After that, it was simply a matter of each of us, Cattousse, Sparks, and me, gradually moving the conversation closer to the delicate, central subject of suitable presents for a censor who was so kind as to seal his ears while we made our overseas calls. It was intimated that, in those difficult days, with food-hoarding sending the prices up, and gasoline hard to get, and the future so uncertain, the most practical presents would be American dollars.

At first Cattousse charged only $10 a call. Then he raised the rate to $5 a minute. We felt it was still a bargain, and we paid. I don't know how many of the other correspondents he took on as clients, but my guess is that he got all of us; while his business lasted, he might easily have been clearing $500 a day. One of the results of this arrangement was a romantic item on my expense account—"bribes to censor: $160." It was paid without question.

Cattousse's sudden wealth caused him immediately to blossom: he appeared wearing a large diamond ring, a gold key chain, a gold tie clip, a new gray and brown plaid suit and yellow snakeskin shoes sharp enough to stab someone with. Sparks and I once took him to lunch. Cattousse was ingenuously enthusiastic about his present circumstances. As he munched through a steak and a strawberry sundae, washed down with Dutch lager and sealed with a double Cointreau, he said:

"You know, man, in these countries it doesn't pay to be fanatic. Middle of the road all the way, that's me."

"You and Eisenhower," Sparks said.

"That's the ticket!" Cattousse jubilantly agreed. "I get along with the government; I get along with you chaps: everybody happy."

As we left the restaurant, I noticed that Cattousse had left a $5 tip on the marble table. His bill could hardly have exceeded $10. He was really living.

"That Cattousse," Sparks gravely commented later "—the man's beginning to spend money with the reckless vulgarity of a correspondent."

We heard American broadcasts from correspondents in Tegucigalpa, Honduras, reporting Castillo Armas's claims of great victories at Chiquimula, Puerto Barrios, and Zacapa, in eastern Guatemala. The Guatemalan Government was claiming defensive triumphs at the same places. As we were not allowed to accompany the Guatemalan army into the field (did it venture into the field?), we were never quite sure whether there was really any substance behind the communiqués, whether in fact there was any fighting going on anywhere at all.

The only indications of hostilities that I myself actually observed throughout the nine-day campaign were the air raids by Nicaraguan Thunderbolts on the capital and the wild, frenzied, totally ineffectual ground fire that the raids provoked. The passage of a plane over the city and the explosion of a couple of small bombs were sufficient to cause haphazard machine-gunning all night in the dark streets. We became accustomed to the whine of bullets ricocheting off the walls of nearby buildings as nervous soldiers and policemen shot at cigarettes and other casual violations of the blackout.

One afternoon I had a private appointment with Ambassador Peurifoy at the U.S. Embassy. When I got there I was told he was on the roof. I joined him. He was wearing a one-piece flying suit and looking through field glasses into the eastern sky. Soon I heard the drone of a single-engine plane, and then saw it flying our way about 2,000 feet above the ground.

"Wouldn't it be a good idea to take cover?" I suggested.

"It's all right," Peurifoy assured me, as he checked his watch. "They're going for the Aurora gasoline storage tanks. We'll be all right here." Not surprisingly, he proved to be correct. This was a well managed revolution.

Sparks, by chance, had established contact with two Harvard University undergraduates who were passing through Guatemala in the course of a vacation trip along the Pan-American Highway. They were driving an MG sports car, which was laden with U.S. Army surplus equipment, such as sleeping bags and a shovel with which to dig the car out of the mud. The two young men had driven from the Mexican border through numerous roadblocks at which they had been searched but not harmed by Indians with machetes. We made an appointment to interview the students at their hotel in Guatemala City.

The reception clerk looked at us nervously as he led the way to their room. The door was half open. We went in.

The two students were sitting on one of the beds. The room was full of "secret" police, whose arrogant, bullying manner transcended the disguise of civilian dress.

"What seems to be the trouble?" Sparks asked one of the students.

"They think—" he began to explain.

"Silence!" ordered an oily-haired man with skin like beaten copper. "You," he said to Sparks, "sit down." The policeman pointed to the other bed.

"How dare you behave like this?" Sparks protested angrily, shaking his untidily furled umbrella in the policeman's face. Sparks always carried an umbrella in trouble spots because, as he had put it, "nobody ever hits a man carrying an umbrella."

"Do you know who Señor Catling and I have just been talking to?" he demanded. "Your foreign minister, that's who. He promised that the foreign press was to be allowed to move about unmolested. The press—*periodistas*, you jerk. Foreign minister—Toriello—*palacio*—understand?" He turned to me exasperatedly. "Don't they understand anything?"

The policeman seemed not to understand; but perhaps he had caught the name Toriello, for he became perceptibly more formal. He asked us to sit down—"please," and added in Spanish of which I got only the gist that another police officer soon would arrive to assume charge of the investigation, a police officer who spoke English.

We sat quietly on the beds, waiting, while two junior officers stuffed the students' belongings into their kit bags. Then we heard sharp footsteps across the tiles of the patio, the door opened wide, and in strode Gerald Cattousse. When he saw us prisoners he looked as though he might faint.

After a small convulsion of the features, however, he managed to compose his face in an expression of non-recognition. Being in the middle, not fully committed to either side, he was feeling the opposite pressures of salary and bribes. We were at his mercy, we realized; but he also was at ours, and we felt that he knew it. There was a moment of tense uncertainty as unstated threats and promises passed silently but forcefully like electric charges from mind to mind across the small room.

Cattousse, with the histrionic ability of a six-year-old child, assumed a manner of efficiency and severity, while pleading with his eyes for tolerance and cooperation. It occurred to me that it would have been a lot simpler for everyone concerned if he had identified us; but possibly he welcomed a chance to prove his loyalty to the régime by assisting at an arrest, even an unjustified one.

"The penalty for espionage at a time like this is death," he said. "You are suspected of spying and passing information to your friends at this rendezvous. You must come to Guardia Civil headquarters." He took me firmly by the elbow and led the way out of the room. "It's all right," he whispered hoarsely, "I'll telephone the embassy."

Then, "All right," he said in an unnaturally loud voice, "let's go. No tricks now."

A policeman was trying without success to start the students' MG. The students themselves were not to be trusted in it. I offered to drive it. There was a consultation. I was allowed to get into the driver's seat, covered first by an officer on the sidewalk and then by another sitting beside me with a pistol shoved, B-movie-fashion, against my ribs. Sparks and the students were escorted on foot. It started to rain. Sparks's umbrella had been taken away, and he looked furious.

Within three-quarters of an hour, the first secretary came over from the embassy.

"What," he said to me, "you again?"

Nothing had happened to us in custody. Another apology would be conveyed from the palace to the embassy. But Sparks and I had both experienced an uneasy sensation that the situation might be closing in on us. What might have happened if Cattousse had not shown up? What if conditions got worse and junior agents of the police began to make decisions of their own? We sat in the lobby of the Pan-American and contemplated flight from the country.

"We could write the first 'Now-it-can-be-told' stories," he pointed out.

"I don't think if I had a chance to tell all I know I'd have very much to tell," I admitted.

"There's plenty," Sparks said.

We considered taking a train to Tapachula, Mexico; but the trains had no diners or club cars. We considered disguising ourselves as sacks of coffee and riding on a truck to the Pacific port of San José and thence in a Japanese freighter (the *Something Maru* was loading) to Yokohama and thence. . . . The route would be difficult to explain to our editors.

"Anyway, I can't go," Sparks said. "I've got laundry out. It includes a bush jacket from Abercrombie's."

"*Life* magazine has bought a case of embassy Scotch," I added.

"We'd better stay."

"We can go over to the palace and give Toriello hell in the morning. That always produces some sort of story."

We complained to the foreign minister daily until the government fell and he sought asylum, with Palmieri, Gutierrez, Arbenz, and the rest of his colleagues.

The revolution had been a long one. It had lasted nine days. It had given the government plenty of time to clean out the treasury. It had given a local manufacturer time to make Army of Liberation T-shirts in which the populace could demonstrate its new loyalty when Castillo Armas's mob hit town.

Castillo observed the Latin-American tradition of granting safe-conduct passes out of the country to enemies who had gained asylum in sympathetic foreign embassies. New governments are lenient in this way because today's ins may be next year's outs: one's opponents' escape routes are kept open for oneself. The system minimizes casualties and helps to perpetuate the revolutionary and counterrevolutionary spirits of the country.

The whole affair seemed less amiable when the anti-Communist prisoners told their stories about the tortures and executions of the last few days of the Arbenz régime. Horribly mutilated bodies were dug up and displayed. Some of them, though not long buried, could be identified only by their dentists.

Just before Castillo's arrival, Gerald Cattousse managed to get himself arrested and beaten up. When he got out of the hospital he went to the United States Embassy and asked Harold Urist, the public affairs officer, to lend him $20. Cattousse said he felt he deserved some compensation as a martyr in the cause of freedom of the press. Urist said he was sorry, he didn't have $20 to spare for this purpose.

Cattousse came again to us correspondents.

"I've got a terrific idea," he said. "I'm going to organize a Negro tourist agency. I'll allow my friends to invest in it."

But times had changed. There was a new chief of police, there was no censorship, and Cattousse no longer seemed to have any friends.

Ex-President Arbenz got to his ancestral country, Switzerland, with a fortune of several million dollars.

162

Castillo Armas became president and in due course was assassinated.

I don't know who is the president of Guatemala as I write now. It probably doesn't make much difference who he is. The place has a wonderful climate, anyway.

27

After the victory parade, the speeches, the toasts, and the post-
mortem political analyses, I was free to continue my tour of Central
America. Several correspondents, myself among them, discovered
compelling reasons for flying to Mexico City, which is one of the elegant cities of the world, and which was particularly attractive that
summer because the government had just drastically devalued the
peso. As we separated at Mexico City airport, I felt a slight pang of
regret that the camaraderie of the revolution was at an end. However, there were consolations in the prospect before us: the broad
boulevards, the rococo fountains, the skyscrapers, the flowers, the
Parisian dresses, the tequila cocktails on the roof of the Bamer Hotel.

Clay Felker, then a reporter for *Life*, and I soon flew to the coast
for a weekend of water-skiing at Acapulco. We took a hotel villa on
a high promontory overlooking the Pacific Ocean. Before allowing
myself to go down to the beach, I settled in a chaise longue on a terrace beside the hotel swimming pool, with a planter's punch at my
elbow, and completed my last Guatemalan expense accounts.

This display of puritanical stoicism so aggravated Felker, who was accustomed to the irresponsible ways of his own craft, that he sneaked up behind me and tipped me into the water. The planter's punch was damaged beyond repair, my accounts fluttered about in all directions, and I was obliged to dive to the bottom of the pool to retrieve my sunglasses. Worst of all, I noticed as I climbed back to the terrace that I was still wearing my wrist watch, a Longines that I had bought in Natal eleven years before. It had marked the time with perfect, astronomical exactitude; it could be expected to do so no longer. Even though I kept my head, and a waiter with all dispatch brought a pat of butter ("the best butter"), the watch since then has always behaved with unpredictable eccentricity. I just want to get it on record that it was Felker's fault, not Latin America's, that I returned to the efficient North with a reduced capacity for punctuality.

Three U.S. Navy destroyer escorts, on training cruises, called at Acapulco for recreation on the way back to their base in California. They had just achieved an obscure and complicatedly qualified "first": they were the first units of the Pacific Fleet to have made an easterly transit of the Panama Canal for seven years. In the brain-softening sunshine of Acapulco, this distinction seemed worth recording. Besides, the customary plea for men from Maryland produced an ensign and a hospital corpsman. Any old story was publishable if it included some local names.

The weekend went on a bit. At last, though, Felker had to go back to New York. I spent a couple of days in Mexico City, studying the economic situation, to which, I felt, I had already become a considerable contributing factor. The article I wrote on Mexican economics was not very interesting, but it was very, very long: it had a good, gray, serious appearance on the page.

I worked out a routine for the rest of my tour. In each microcosmic capital, I spent the first day calling on whichever diplomats or consular officials were available, the second day I talked with leaders of the political opposition, the third day I interviewed the leader of the government, the fourth day I played golf or swam with local businessmen, the fifth day I wrote authoritatively on The Situation; and the sixth day I packed my suitcase and moved on to the next place.

There may be other regions of the world where presidents are more approachable, the scenery is more beautiful, the sun is brighter, the lines of controversy more clearly defined, the people more amiable, the distances shorter, and the datelines more colorful, and where foreign correspondence is more easily, pleasantly, and inexpensively conducted than in Central America; but I cannot imagine where.

After visiting Belize and Tegucigalpa, I reached Managua, Nicaragua, just as President Don Anastasio Somoza was announcing, in the words of another dictator who came to an inglorious end, that his patience was exhausted. It had been exhausted, he said, by his southern neighbor, President José María Figueres, of Costa Rica. President Somoza made it known that if there were any further "provocation" he would have no alternative but to order his army to move across the San Juan River, which divided the two unfriendly republics. Costa Rican police had fired at river boats that were carrying some fugitive bank robbers; President Somoza called them "Costa Rican revolutionaries." The boats had been carrying them to the "privileged sanctuary" north of the river.

I arranged for an appointment, and a taxi took me up the long hill to the presidential palace, a vast building heavily guarded by soldiers.

President Somoza was sitting in an armchair in the center of the main foyer, a room about the size of an average movie theater. Guards with submachine guns stood in all the doorways. Some of the guards were looking out of the foyer; others were looking into it. The president, a brawny man in his late fifties with a fat but tough-looking face, was wearing a tropical khaki uniform that bore on its shoulders the five-star insignia of the chief director of the Nicaraguan National Guard. He was smoking a cigarette in a long silver and ebony holder, reminiscent of the man he said was his idol, the late Franklin D. Roosevelt.

I told President Somoza that I had just come from Guatemala, where it had been supposed that some of the "rebel" bombing had been done by Nicaraguan planes. Was that true? He chuckled until his swarthy jowls quivered and his medals clinked.

"Let us put it this way," he said, "we have the finest air force in Central America. The United States and Nicaragua are good friends.

We are both against the Communists. When we Nicaraguans can do anything to help our friends, they have only to ask us."

I asked him whether there was any Communist danger in Nicaragua. Again he looked amused.

"You haven't been here before, have you?" he said. "There is no internal threat. Nicaraguans, thank God, are a hundred per cent loyal. But you know, don't you, that there has been a very immediate Communist threat to the whole of Central America, the whole Hemisphere?

"My own miraculous escape from assassination last April was the first breakdown in the Communist plot to take over Central America. After taking over Nicaragua, the Communists were going to paralyze Honduras with strikes against the fruit companies. The third phase was to be the final communization of Guatemala. And then Communist agents from Mexico and Guatemala were going to finish the rest—and there would have gone your Panama Canal. . . .

"They almost got me," he said, shaking his head in awe at the recollection. He had canceled at the last minute a scheduled appearance at a dinner at the International Club, and, because of a sudden whim, wanting to see the Argentine race horses on his eastern ranch, he had canceled the usual weekend visit to his Pacific Coast sugar plantation and salt refinery. His agents had subsequently discovered that there had been gunmen at the dinner and gunmen on the road to the Pacific Coast, he said.

"The situation in Central America is much better now. The only remaining danger is Figueres. Figueres is unpredictable from day to day and must be watched.

"When you talk to Figueres he walks up and down with his finger to his forehead and a faraway look in his eyes. He thinks he's a visionary and he's looking for visions.

"Figueres has a Napoleon complex. The people around him have managed to convince him that Central America should be unified under his leadership.

"Bull-shit!" said the president. He drew an ivory-handled knife from his belt and tested its blade with a thumb.

"You know what Figueres is? He's a lousy Commie. But he's

167

only a small one." Somoza grinned and leaned forward and gently tapped my knee with the blade of the knife. "He's so small and he wants to be so big he wears built-up shoes. You're going to Costa Rica? Good. You wait. When you go there, you look at Figueres' shoes. You'll see that I'm telling the truth."

President Somoza's son-in-law, Nicaragua's ambassador to Washington, Guillermo Sevilla Sacasa, who was home on vacation, put his arm around my shoulder and told me: "The basic question is this: does Figueres want friendship or does he want animosity? Does he want honey or does he want vinegar? President Somoza has a plentiful supply of both."

I was sent back to my hotel in a black, bulletproof limousine. During the short drive I reflected that Somoza's Figueres syllogism evidently went like this.

1. Somoza is an anti-Communist.
2. Figueres is anti-Somoza.
3. Therefore, Figueres is a Communist.

I went to see President Figueres.

He wasn't in San José, the capital of Costa Rica, when I sought an audience. He was visiting Puerto Limón, on the Caribbean coast. I followed him there.

He was reclining on a sofa in his small bedroom in the provincial Government House when he received me. He put down a copy of *The Atlantic Monthly,* in which he had been reading an article by Hanson Baldwin entitled "Churchill Was Right." President Figueres' political orientation coincided more closely with Attlee's than with Churchill's, but Figueres said: "A very good article, very well written."

The president was a small, neat man of early middle age. He had receding black hair, a long nose, a short upper lip and a Victor Borge smile. It was true that his tiny pointed shoes seemed extraordinarily thick-soled.

"I would be willing to attend any meeting that could resolve the differences between Nicaragua and my country," he said. "But there are no real political issues. Somoza doesn't want to end the friction, for the simple reason that he's using it as a distraction from domestic dissatisfaction at a time when he's getting the Nicaraguan Constitution amended so that he can succeed himself yet again as president.

"At the same time Somoza claims the people of Costa Rica are dissatisfied with our government and that by scaring them he can cause revolts. What he doesn't seem to realize is that Costa Rica isn't ruled by a dictatorship like his. The people are in power here. They can't very well revolt against themselves.

"Let's go for a walk," Figueres suggested as though he wished to change the subject. "This will be a peripatetic interview," he said, as he led the way downstairs. "Like Truman's. Peripatetic," he repeated, relishing the word, of which he had been reminded, perhaps, by the *Atlantic*'s peripatetic Mr. Weeks.

Two young men in khaki uniforms jumped to their feet and started to follow us out of the building. They were the president's bodyguards. He casually waved them back to their chairs.

We walked across the street, past a sloth that sat immobile in the middle. Occasional bicycles were steered carefully around the obstacle. Puerto Limón was fond of its sloths. They seemed to enjoy the status of civic mascots.

On the opposite sidewalk, an incredibly ancient Negro like Uncle Remus hobbled quickly up to the president and halted him with a bony hand.

"Pepe," the old man said (Pepe being the Spanish for Joe), "did you get my letter?" The old man spoke English with a Jamaican accent.

"What letter?" the president asked.

"Oh, dear, oh, dear," the old man grumbled. "I knew you didn't get it."

"Perhaps you didn't address it correctly," the president suggested soothingly. "Why don't you try again? You know I always answer all my mail. What was your letter about?"

"I've been having some trouble with the Nicaraguans," the old man said. President Figueres laughed ruefully and sympathetically patted the old man on the back.

"So have I," the president said.

We entered the home of the sloths, a tame jungle or wild park of tall palms and gnarled banyans of immense girth. There was a broken view of blue sea and blue sky. It was a charming place to be president of.

In a leisurely fashion, President Figueres expounded his economic theories and political philosophy in the fluent American-English that he had refined at the Massachusetts Institute of Technology and Columbia University.

He said he favored an international system of commodity price supports, preferably administered by an agency of the United Nations. A world-wide organization should purchase and store surplus raw materials in highly productive years and sell them in years of low productivity, thus stabilizing prices.

He politely deplored American foreign policies based on military expediency. He pointed out that there was little to choose between dictators of the extreme right and dictators of the extreme left.

"Think of Somoza and Chiang Kai-shek and Franco," he said. "Nicaragua and the Dominican Republic and Venezuela are just as bad as Guatemala under Arbenz."

I liked Figueres.

"We must have another talk," he said on our way back to Government House. "The next time we're both in San José, drop around to the palace and meet my wife."

28

After a month's vacation with my wife and daughter in Guatemala and Mexico and a four-month period of local reporting and reviewing movies in Baltimore, I returned to Costa Rica in January, 1955. After months of talk, fighting had broken out on the Costa Rican side of the border between Costa Rica and Nicaragua. Direct flights from the United States to Costa Rica had been temporarily suspended, but I was able to fly from New Orleans to Panama City and from there to San José.

I went to a restaurant where any American correspondents in the country would be likely to have dinner. Sure enough, there was a small group of them, drinking martinis and trying to decide the best way of covering the revolution or war or whatever was taking place in Guancaste Province.

"What are *you* going to do?" one of them asked me with the slight condescension that is sometimes shown by a reporter who has been on the scene of a story twenty-four hours longer than a colleague.

"First," I said, "I'd like to see the menu. Then I think I'll ask President Figueres for his advice."

"Ha, ha," mirthlessly commented my questioner.

"He hasn't been giving press conferences," a kinder veteran explained.

Having placed my order, I excused myself to telephone a number I had been given in Washington. The telephone was attached to the wall within sight of our table. I was eating my soup when the waitress came over and asked for me by name.

"The president wants to speak to you," she said.

It was a great moment, the first of a series of great moments. Thanks to the president's good will, Costa Rica for me was one great moment after another. It was so easy, it seemed like cheating. It was a reporter's dream come true.

"What is it? What's going on?" I was asked when I sat down again. It was nothing, I said; just a personal conversation. I told the waitress to cancel my order for dessert.

"You're on to something," someone bitterly complained. "Is it a Cabinet meeting?"

"The United Nations?"

"Has Nicaragua declared war?"

It was none of those things.

"It's just that Madame Figueres has baked a cake and she wondered if I'd like to go around and try it. Banana cream, I believe."

Of course, nobody was convinced.

The cake was delicious.

Early the next morning, as arranged, I reported to the Presidential Palace as a small convoy was preparing to leave for "the front." I took with me one other correspondent, Christopher Lucas, of the London *Daily Mail*, which had rewarded me quite handsomely for the small amount of help I had been able to give them during the Guatemalan campaign.

Madame Figueres, an attractive blonde Danish-American whom the President had met at Columbia, was standing in the doorway of the palace holding in her arms their month-old son, José María, Jr.

"This is one time I wish I were not a woman," she said. "I told

Pepe I would have my hair cropped, wash off my make-up, and put on a uniform, but he said no. He said there are 10,000 other volunteers."

President Figueres drove his own car. One of his ministers, with a machine-pistol on his lap, sat on the president's right. Lucas and I sat in the back. The rest of the convoy consisted of jeeps loaded with armed men that were to precede and follow the president's car. President and Madame Figueres fondly waved to each other, as a departing commuter might exchange farewells with a suburban housewife, and we headed northwest, up the Pan-American Highway.

The president said that he was encouraged by the Organization of American States' commission, whose investigations in the field had just resulted in a report implicating President Somoza as the instigator of the fighting.

Figueres added, however, that the U.S. Navy Marlin patrol planes that had been sent up from Panama to make observations of the border region for the OAS commission were obviously unable to deter the Nicaraguans. While the Marlins were overhead there were no attacks, but the patrol cover was not continuous; as soon as the Marlins left the scene there were further violations.

"The United States should provide a continuous air patrol of high-speed aircraft authorized to shoot, if necessary," the president said.

"Why don't you ask for that?" I asked, with pencil poised, like a grocer ready to take an order.

"Yes," he said.

"Perhaps an American aircraft carrier could do the job," I suggested.

"That's a good idea."

"But, of course, you really need some planes of your own."

President Figueres frequently stopped the convoy to shake hands and talk with volunteers wearing bandoliers of ammunition over their farm work clothes and carrying antique rifles. At every defensible bend in the road men of the civilian home guard arose from camouflaged strong points in the deep ditches as the convoy approached. Every bridge was guarded. Figueres greeted the volunteers

173

as gratefully as a political candidate greets voters the day before election day.

In villages, crowds gathered around the president's car and cheered him. Lucas and I shared some of the glory. The Costa Ricans evidently assumed that we were high-ranking government supporters.

We stopped for lunch at San Ramón, the president's birthplace, where the demonstrations of loyalty were especially fervent.

While the others ate, I wrote a gaudy account of the president's triumphal journey and an article on Figueres' plea for fighter aircraft. Then, while I ate some chicken and ham salad, Figueres himself walked to the local telegraph office to file my cables. He told the manager that they were to be dispatched as top-priority government messages and relayed without delay from San José to Baltimore. The president also left instructions that any other cables I might file there in future were to be handled in the same way.

I realized that the president might not be pampering me for entirely altruistic reasons, but the experience was nonetheless delightful; to have access to the highest news source in the country would have been gratifying enough, but to be served by the president as chauffeur, interpreter, and messenger boy—this, surely, was the ultimate in journalistic luxury. And the Costa Rican cause, I felt comfortably certain, was a good one.

We arrived at advanced military headquarters, a pink-stuccoed fort in Liberia, late in the afternoon. The president introduced me to the military commander, Colonel Marcel Aguiluz, an old professional warrior of the Caribbean Legion whose incipient black beard, dusty fatigues, bulging cartridge belt, and low-slung holster gave him the appearance of a villain in a Western. But when he shook my hand with a big, hairy, thickly padded paw and grinned he seemed more like a jolly pirate. Still, I was glad he was on our side.

The next day President Figueres was in the fort's communications room, where messages were crackling through the command radio from Costa Rica's forward outpost, a farmhouse north of Santa Rosa, when we heard the rapidly loudening drone of an aircraft and the rattle of machine-gun fire. The fort was being attacked again by an "unidentified" Thunderbolt. I suspected that it came from the same base as the "unidentified" Thunderbolts that had flown, under more respectable auspices, against the Arbenz government of Guatemala. President Figueres said that there was no doubt in his mind that the attacking planes came from Nicaragua.

Costa Rican small arms banged and chattered away ineffectually from the roof of the fort. The Thunderbolt slowly climbed and turned and dived at us again. This time we heard bullets thud into the soft wall across the inner courtyard, where swearing cooks were manning a field kitchen that had been established there to feed the garrison's reinforcements. Again the sound of the plane diminished, and again it became louder. President Figueres was indignant.

"We must get some fast planes to put an end to this," he said.

A National Guard captain saluted the president and urged him to take shelter below the stairs.

"How will I know what's going on, if I leave this room?" Figueres asked.

"But it is possible, sir, that the plane may shoot through the windows."

"We will compromise," the president said. "Look: we will sit on the floor beneath this excellent table."

There was another snarl of the diving plane and a chaos of ground fire, and the president's voice for a moment was inaudible.

". . . procure a tiny air force," he said.

"You should keep saying this publicly," I said with some emotion.

"Yes," he agreed; "certainly. You may quote me in any words you like. Just make this meaning clear: we urgently need some planes. But don't report that I am in Liberia, or Somoza will attack it all the more. He's not a strategist; he's just mad. So far his bombs all seem to have been duds; but you never know, his luck might improve."

Perhaps because it was running out of fuel—it did not seem to have been disturbed in the least by our defenses—the Thunderbolt at last turned north. The cooks were able to return to their cauldrons and we were able to emerge, rather stiff-legged, from under the table. The president occupied himself with maps and I did some typing.

Daniel Oduber, Secretary General of President Figueres' National Liberation Party (who had gone on patrol wearing, among other things, a green pork pie hat and a hand grenade), and eighteen other Costa Ricans fought their way out of a Nicaraguan ambush near the border and got back to Liberia with a story that six American correspondents who had been with them had been taken prisoners.

Oduber said he was sure they were all right, so I was able with a clear conscience to enjoy the removal of most of my competitors.

Lucas and I accompanied the president back to San José. On the way, he said he would write out an order entitling me to a government Land-Rover (the British equivalent of a jeep), which we would be able to drive back to the northwest whenever we chose to do so.

When I telephoned the president the next day he was jubilant.

"It's wonderful!" he exclaimed. "We're going to El Coco Airport. In about one hour we shall receive four American fighter planes— F-51 Mustangs! Mustangs are very fast, aren't they?"

"A lot faster than Thunderbolts," I assured him. "Mustangs have Rolls Royce Merlin engines."

"Rolls Royce!" the president marveled. "Wonderful! You must come to meet them. Ambassador Woodward will be there too."

Robert F. Woodward, the U.S. Ambassador, had reported to the State Department that a United States observation plane had been fired on, over Costa Rica, but was undamaged. The OAS observers had reported air attacks against almost defenseless Costa Rican targets. Recommendations that the United States should supply fighter aircraft to Costa Rica might, I suppose, have been going through various channels. However, I had my own theory about the sequence of recent events.

The crucial moment, as I envisioned it, occurred when Secretary of State John Foster Dulles, over breakfast the day before, had read in the Baltimore *Sun* President Figueres' anguished plea for defensive air power. Even though his mouth might have been full of toast, Dulles must have grabbed for a telephone and called the White House.

"Ike," Dulles must have said. "Have you read Catling's article— President Figueres' request for planes?"

"Of course I have, Foster," President Eisenhower must have replied. "I was going to call you. What do you think?"

"A persuasive case. I think we ought to send help," Dulles must have advised.

"I think so too," President Eisenhower must have said. "I'll get onto Defense about it right away. Whew! I don't know what we'd do without that Catling."

"Me neither," Dulles must have confessed.

The rest is history.

President Figueres, Madame Figueres and the entire Costa Rican cabinet were at El Coco to greet the incoming Texas Air National Guard Mustangs.

"They're beautiful, beautiful, beautiful!" the president's wife cried out, so excited that she forgot to take pictures with her new movie camera.

"Here's the four bucks for our air force," the finance minister said to President Figueres.

"I don't think we're going to have to raise the price of coffee to pay for them!" the president replied. "But look how fast they fly!"

Hostile military aircraft were not seen again over Costa Rica. With the help of the Mustangs, flown by Costa Rican pilots, the land fighting was successfully concluded within three days.

I flew up to Managua for another interview with President Somoza and asked him what he thought of the United States' having supplied Costa Rica with planes.

"I resent it," President Somoza said.

His complaint was music to my ears.

Since then he, too, has succumbed to an assassin's bullets.

29

My next domestic interlude on *The Sun* included a few months of writing editorials. *The Sun* still classifies itself as an Independent Democratic newspaper, although it has not supported a Democratic candidate for the Presidency since Roosevelt's second term. The paper's policy is cautiously conservative, except in its occasional liberal concessions to other nations' colonies. Like many other reporters on most major American newspapers, I found myself out of harmony with many opinions expressed on the editorial page. However, as the most junior of editorial writers, I was not required to write on any political subjects of importance, and I was able to maintain an illusion of integrity by regarding the experience as a literary exercise.

For a short time, at least, I was amused by my own pomposity: I assumed in my prose the slow, deliberate, heavy-breathing manner of Colonel Blimp, appraising with controlled outrage or benign condescension such matters as the production of synthetic gasoline from peanuts, the trend in gubernatorial proclamations, the decline of the stork, the growth of the Shakespeare industry, the principle that finders are keepers, and an electrical device for repelling barnacles from ships' bottoms.

The hours were pleasant. We (the editorial "we") arrived at our air-conditioned cubicle, a cell in a row of cells, at about 10:30 in the morning and read the newspapers in time for a conference in the editor's office before a leisurely luncheon. The man who was editor at the time was a decent, kind man who was no longer young. The conference was usually a one-sided affair. The editor gently but firmly imposed his prejudices on a variety of topics and then we carried them to our typewriters for processing by the end of the afternoon. It was possible to leave the office by 5 o'clock. The routine was a restful one, and I detected in myself a comfortable broadening of the rump, a deepening of the jowls. I might have come to regard myself as a leader of the community if my salary had been substantially more than it was, $120 a week. Middle-class penury saved me from the sin of pride.

Late in the summer of 1955, I returned to the local reporting staff. After the austere discipline of the editorial chambers, I enjoyed the anarchy of preparing feature articles. There were occasional days of preposterous invention and rich fantasy, which helped to compensate for the gray days of obituaries and sermons on civic works.

Bishop Charles Manuel Sweet Daddy Grace, an itinerant millionaire Negro evangelist, baptized me (and some others) with a firehose. Miss Gloria Vanderbilt told me about her love poems ("Happiness a wing ding is . . ."). James Margaritis, the proprietor of a bar close to *The Sun*, consented to donate to Mayor D'Alesandro the deeds to five acres on the scenic southwest corner of the great lunar crater Copernicus, and Baltimore thus became the first city in the United States to possess a municipal park on the Moon. (The Mayor, in turn, conferred upon me a certificate of merit, given under the golden-paper corporate seal of the City of Baltimore. This document designated me "an honored and outstanding citizen of Baltimore, worthy of high recognition for . . . contributions to the civic welfare of our municipality.") I boarded the U.S.S. *Constellation*, an antique frigate, in a rented nineteenth century captain's uniform, a photographer made a double exposure, and the resultant picture of a ghost on the quarterdeck was used, obscurely, in the cause of naval recruiting: no medals.

What with one thing and another, it was hardly surprising when the managing editor said he felt it was time that I should be going abroad again. And this time he gave me the assignment I had been yearning for.

30

If anyone ever were to ask me what newspaper assignment to aim for, I would recommend, without hesitation, the post of London correspondent of the Baltimore *Sun*. I would add a warning that the job is such a gratifying one that it leads almost inevitably to subsequent anticlimax. This was the job to which I was assigned in February, 1956. From the very beginning to the very end, I regarded it as pleasanter even than the ideal job proposed by Huntington Cairns, the Washington lawyer and aesthetician, who said he wished he could be the Inspector of Winds and Sunsets, Kitty Hawk (N.C.) Division.

The Sun's London correspondent is given the resounding title of Chief of the London Bureau; but his administrative responsibilities are not exhausting. The bureau consists of two small rooms in the Reuter building at 85 Fleet Street. The staff consists of himself and a woman who orders the sherry, opens the mail, confects the monthly accounts, and writes occasional articles, usually about seasonal fashion shows and the affairs of the royal family. The name of my assistant was Joan Graham. The bureau was equipped also with telephones, a Reuter teleprinter, a dictionary, a set of the *Encyclopaedia Britannica*, Dodd's *Parliamentary Companion*, some maps, and a number of drinking glasses and recent editions of *Vogue* and *Country Life*. The Burgundy-red wall-to-wall carpeting, the oyster-gray walls, the black desks and armchairs, the circular glass table, and the color photographs of English rural scenes have reminded Gerard Fay, the London editor of the Manchester *Guardian*, of "the offices of a minor airline." As I designed the décor, I have disagreed with him. Anyway, the title of Chief of Bureau, even though it's a tiny bureau, gives the correspondent equal status, if not equal stature, to that of any other foreign correspondent in London. Though the man from *The Sun* may not attain the majesty and prestige of the New York *Times* Chief of Bureau or the power of the Chief of Bureau of the Associated Press, he can expect to enjoy the same rights and privileges as they do, the same entrée into government offices, the same invitations to Buckingham Palace garden parties and to the innumerable press conferences that illuminate the life of the capital.

There were many other local advantages for a correspondent representing an American newspaper. Greenwich Mean Time is five hours, sometimes six, ahead of Eastern Standard Time. The language spoken in England, as the British Travel Association has taken such pains to point out, is English. London is the greatest newspaper city on earth, in the sense that more newspapers of national circulation and international significance are published there than anywhere else. It's almost impossible to miss a major news story there, unless everyone else misses it also, and then it really isn't news, because news is what is reported. London performs for Britain the important characteristic functions that Washington, New York, New Orleans, San Francisco, and Hollywood together perform for the United States. London is the center of British politics, finance, commerce, society, and all the arts, including cookery and jazz. Not the least important benign factor during my tour of duty was the favorable rate of exchange of the dollar and the pound sterling, in terms of local purchasing power.

When I left Baltimore for London, a few days after my thirty-first birthday, my salary was still only $122.50 a week. I could hardly look in the eye the elder of my two brothers, Timothy, who was seven years younger than I, yet already threatening to become an advertising tycoon; for that matter, it wasn't particularly easy to meet the gaze of my younger brother, Duncan, who was earnestly engaged in systematic scholarship and was clearly determined to break a family tradition of half a century by earning his B.A.

But in New York, on the eve of sailing to Southampton, I was notified by the managing editor that he had been able to raise the amount to $130, or $7.50 a week above the minimum journeyman's wage provided then by the paper's contract with the American Newspaper Guild. And on arrival in London, I was immediately paid an extra $62.50 a week "cost of living allowance," although the cost of living in London is lower than the cost of living in Baltimore. Furthermore, I was provided with an office car. It was a humble Ford Anglia, but worth at least, say, $17.50 a week, including gas and oil, maintenance and insurance and membership in the Automobile Association. Finally, I was, of course, entitled to spend office funds on all expenses directly connected with my work—for example, the cost of taking Members of Parliament out to lunch, or the cost of spending a week at the Edinburgh Festival. In addition to the funds that had to be accounted for in some detail, there was a box of money in the office safe for little incidentals such as taxis and theater tickets.

In short, after having been one of the poorest people I knew, I had suddenly become one of the relatively wealthy ones, living at a level of at least $15,000 a year. "If it's good enough for the Prime Minister," I used to say, "it's good enough for me."

Nearly ten years had passed since the last time I had left London. I returned with the nostalgia of a native and the wide-eyed enthusiasm of a friendly alien. I had lived there before as a schoolboy and had stayed there as a navigator on leave; now I was able to penetrate the life of the place more generally and more intimately, partly because I was an adult and a civilian, principally because I was a journalist.

Although all classes of people in London are voracious readers of newspapers, reporters as a group are not universally respected there. They haven't the high standing that reporters can attain in Washington. On the whole, Britons are less sophisticated and calculating than Americans about the ways and means of achieving favorable relations with the public. Die-hards in London still resist invasions of privacy.

Vulgarity in the press is deplored as often as it occurs—daily. Libel actions are taken against newspapers for offensive allegations that would pass almost unnoticed in Broadway columns—and British juries tend to favor the plaintiffs in this sort of case. But in spite of certain reservations and resistances, London nowadays opens most of its doors to newspapermen; and the more important doors seem to open more easily than some of the lesser ones.

I crossed the Atlantic alone, in the *Queen Elizabeth*. There were elaborate, vinous meals in the Veranda Grill that reminded me, before the end of the five-day voyage, of the Pont cartoon of a sulky débutante despondently looking down at her plate and saying: "Gosh! Quails in aspic again." But English cuisine, or French cuisine under English auspices, had made some spectacular progress since the lean days of rabbit pie and dehydrated eggs, and so somehow I forced down all the truffles and béarnaise sauce and brandy butter.

In the vast, almost empty lounges, elderly couples in evening dress put on spurious paper-hat gaiety for bingo and horse racing. Middle-aged businessmen just back from selling tweed and motorcycles in the Middle West stood at the bar deriding American folkways. I met Derek Marks, a young man of Chestertonian avoirdupois, then the political correspondent of the London *Daily Express*, who, according to the late Charlie Campbell, director of British Information Service in Washington, had an extraordinary grasp of parliamentary intrigue. But one of the businessmen had latched onto Marks before the ship had slipped her moorings in the East River. There were no briefings on the latest maneuverings in the House of Commons, only the loud laughter of a salesman on a spree.

But the crossing had its charms. I abstained from ping-pong, and found a copy of A. G. Macdonnell's *England, Their England*. I sat in a remote chair with whisky and soda and read and reread the wonderful chapter about the village cricket match. This chapter had been poignant during my years away from England; now it was joyous.

The man I was succeeding, Bradford Jacobs, was charitably doing all the writing during my first three weeks in London. I was supposed to be getting acquainted with the place. It is a gray city of Portland stone darkened by soot and weathered pale at the edges; the parks are green, even in winter; the great streets are animated with black taxis and red buses, as handsome as ceremonial military parades. I saw it all so fresh, gloriously glittering, that I wondered why I had stayed away so long.

While gaslights were popping into flame in the blue dusk of late afternoon, I called on Dr. W. R. Matthews, the dean of St. Paul's, and Mrs. Matthews, at the deanery, which was built by Wren.

"I remember the time," said Mrs. Matthews as she carefully sliced through lemon icing, "when an architect warned me that the house might at any moment collapse—and the Queen Mother was expected to tea. 'How awful it would be,' I thought, 'if the Queen Mother were to fall through the floor into the kitchen sink.' I'm sure she would have been most gracious about it, but she might not have come to tea again."

I heard about the credit squeeze from bankers at their port and Stilton in the cheerful fug of the George & Vulture, a small seventeenth century chophouse in the City; there were conversations with Foreign Office information men over Aylesbury duck at Simpson's; with R. H. S. Crossman, M.P., over pink gins in the House of Commons; with Frank Allaun, M.P., in a restaurant in Soho ("do you realize that this dinner is costing more than most of my constituents earn in a whole week?" he asked balefully as the waiter refilled his glass); with Julian Amery, M.P., in his library (on the chimneypiece was a reminder of "a danger we mustn't forget," a photograph of an Egyptian chess player, President Gamal Abdel Nasser).

I drove the dusty pea-green Anglia up Downing Street and through a dark archway into the Foreign Office courtyard and parked beside official black limousines.

Two policemen watched disinterestedly as I lifted and dropped the heavy metal knocker against the plain black door of Number 10. The door opened and I went in, as easily as in a dream, though I wasn't carrying a red dispatch box or a dark brief case or even wearing a bowler hat.

William Clarke, Prime Minister Sir Anthony Eden's press secretary, received me in his small, plainly elegant office.

How was Patrick O'Donovan getting on in Washington? Clarke

wondered. Had I had a smooth crossing? Did I find London cold? Would I prefer tea or coffee? Black or white? Sugar?

The room for a moment was silent, except for the delicate chink of silver against china. Clarke fingered fastidiously the knot of his gray silk tie.

"Incidentally," he said, "you've come at an interesting time. Actually, there's a sort of crisis. The Jordanians have just sacked Glubb."

It was ominous that my first article from London was an account of the ousting of Lieutenant General John Bagot Glubb from command of the Arab Legion. Although I was now a London correspondent and wanted nothing more than to preoccupy myself with the immediate surroundings, I was no better able than Britain itself to avoid spending much, and then more, and then almost all of the time considering the growing threats of Arab nationalists in the Middle East.

Eden gave a small cocktail party for American correspondents a short time afterward. As he urbanely sipped a dry martini, he chatted about the Middle East as though it had been bad weather or a disease.

He told the House of Commons that if the government abandoned Cyprus as a military base Britain would have no way of protecting its Middle Eastern oil interests, the Suez Canal, and the integrity of Israel and Jordan. Without Middle Eastern oil, he said, Britain would suffer unemployment and starvation.

A few weeks later he told some of us that the Middle East had been the gravest subject of discussion with Premier Nikolai A. Bulganin and Nikita S. Khrushchev when they had visited him. If anyone interfered with Britain's access to its main sources of oil, Eden said, Britain would fight. It was not easy to realize that he meant just what he said.

There was still time for minor pleasures. I reported Lord Windlesham's lament for the decline of practical joking, the Icelandic general election, the opening of a hospital in St. Lô, the Henley Royal Regatta, the advent of Marilyn Monroe, the Anglo–New Zealand croquet test matches and Nina Ponomareva's theft of five hats from a West End store. I tried to learn about British domestic politics and economics.

But all this and a lot more were swept aside by events on a larger scale. Soon after President Nasser expropriated the Suez Canal, I flew to Cairo. The diplomats were still talking, but preparations were being made for war.

31

"Speak to me not as an American to an Egyptian," begged Sayed El Gabry, proprietor of Azhar Bazaar, a small Cairo gift shop that specialized in brass trays and embroidered cushions.

"We are both human," he said. "Speak to me the truth, as brother to brother. Will there be war?"

His shop looked so desolate—I was the only potential customer—that I hadn't the heart to talk about the growing concentration at Aldershot of tanks painted the color of the desert, the paratroops clambering aboard air transports at Blackbushe aerodrome, the naval reinforcements at Malta, the troops alerted on Cyprus.

"No war," I said. "Everything will be fixed by talking."

"No war!" he echoed. He seized upon the assurance. "That is what the Congressman from the Philippines said yesterday. War is truly bad for everybody; everybody knows it."

The merchant clapped together his brown hands, as though ordering a celebration. A few moments later a barefoot young man in a white gown and a brown skullcap slapped into the dim back room with a salver bearing glasses of bright yellow lemonade for me and my guide.

"It is hospitality," said our host. "There is no charge. You have made me very glad. The situation will improve this week? Business is very bad for us now. But soon Gamal Abdel Nasser will make everything all right."

"Hmmm," I said. "How much are the dressing gowns?" The rare moment of human sympathy had ended and we began the traditional probe and withdrawal of Oriental bargaining.

Moses, the "Official Dragoman," a splendid figure of a man with distinguished gray hair and a grand nose and the sticky persistence of a horsefly, guided me away from the bazaar to visit pyramids and mosques.

We drove out to Mena House for lunch. The last time I had been there, during the war, genial Egyptian racketeers with gold teeth and white dinner jackets and British generals with their beautiful mistresses had been dancing on the terrace. Now the place was empty except for waiters in white gowns, red fezzes, and red cummerbunds, standing about waiting for people to wait on.

I relayed the bazaar proprietor's anxious question to the Sphinx, and the Sphinx told me as much as I had learned from the Ministry of National Guidance.

Moses took me to the Mohammed Ali Mosque and preached against the decadence of ex-King Farouk. From a broad parapet we looked down on a low-lying panorama of grayish-ochre buildings and the brownish Nile glimmering mercurially through heat haze.

"One day," Moses said proudly, "we have new dam, all you see covered with water, grow plenty food, everybody live in nice new house in the mountains with air condition. Maybe twenty years."

We walked past children with bandaged eyes and beggars lying on the ground with their knees drawn up like embryos'. Moses spoke sharply to an old man who held out a supplicatory hand, and we got back into the car.

We politely encouraged each other. I doubt that Sayed El Gabry had really believed my assurance of peace; and I did not believe Moses' assurance of plenty; but we were kind to each other, and kindness itself helped to get one through difficult days.

After my last infrared treatment in a Catholic hospital for a poisonous bite that I had suffered when sitting on a spider, I arranged to go on to Suez. I was supposed to be doing feature articles while staying close to the probable center of future events.

A taxi took me southeast across the desert to Port Tewfik, the southern terminus of the Suez Canal.

Fortunately, the British consul there was an old acqaintance, Joseph Mulvenny, who had served as the consul in Baltimore for several years. British women and children had already been sent home, and there were many vacant rooms in his dazzling white new consulate on the west bank of the canal.

"Sitting on my balcony, I can see both Africa and Asia," he pointed out in the flat voice of a man who had long since tired of the view. Egyptian police in crumpled white uniforms leaned on their rifles in the shade of palms like feather dusters.

"I give them cigarettes," Mulvenny said. "They're not bad fellows. But we're beginning to get a bit irritable. It hasn't rained for ten months. The midday temperature recently reached 114." Mulvenny mopped his red brow at the thought. "The mango tree that the Bishop of Egypt planted when he dedicated the consulate last spring is still all right, but if we have to leave I doubt that the Gyppos will water it. Shall we have a whisky?"

British shipping agents and oil company engineers came over for dinner. One of the agents made some telephone calls and arranged to get me aboard a ship that would be heading for Port Said the following day. We all went to the French Club, abandoned but for the bartender and the waiters, and we had a pessimistic party in the patio.

"This used to be very gay," Mulvenny said.

I ordered araq, an Arabic liquor that tastes something like Pernod, but worse.

"If only they'd play some music."

"The orchestra has broken up."

"They've got a loudspeaker system."

"How about requesting 'Nearer My God to Thee'?"

But the first record, played very loud, was "Rock Around the Clock."

Soviet-built MIG's of the Egyptian Air Force were whistling overhead the next day as the Norwegian tanker *Vinga* sailed slowly northward.

The master allowed me to sit on the bridge. I was going to do a story on piloting a ship through the canal. The British and French pilots having left Egypt, the job was being done by Egyptians, who were training newcomers from the Soviet Union and the United States to help keep the ships moving.

The *Vinga* was piloted by Ismail Rafeek, of Cairo. Fedor Penkov, of Odessa, was under instruction. Rafeek was short and stocky. He was wearing a white shirt and long white shorts and was smoking a pipe: he looked like a games master in an inferior English school. Penkov had the mournful face of George Orwell and long white linen trousers; he looked like an intellectual barber. But it was no use inwardly ridiculing their appearance. They were proficient navigators. The master of the ship said dispassionately that they were as good as any other pilots. He suggested that it would be unwise to count on the Egyptians to fail as administrators of the canal.

The scene did not seem real. It seemed like a bad dream of the future. But the Russian and the Egyptian were actual; the imperial waterway was under their control; and the time was the present.

Port Said was even more depressing. I took a taxi to Cairo and a plane to Jordan.

In Jerusalem, a guide said that it could not be predicted how long the props and scaffolding would be able to maintain the Church of the Holy Sepulcher. Since the crisis there had been few pilgrims, and, he added pointedly, few donations. I don't know which crisis he meant. The church was dark and smelled of incense, warm wax, and urine.

John Walters, of the London *Daily Mirror*, and I drove to Bethlehem.

"Business is very bad here," said Bishara Canavati, the mayor, director of the Bethlehem Chamber of Commerce, and president of the Bethlehem Lions Club. "Last year we had a quarter million visitors —28,000 Americans. Wonderful year. They spent plenty money, bought plenty things."

If it hadn't been for his export business (he supplied U.S. Army PX's from Frankfurt to Tokyo), he said, his souvenir factory might have had to close down. As things were, he had already been obliged to get rid of some of the girls on the assembly line where the mother-of-pearl crucifixes were made.

"We hoped Point Four Program would build a nice big hotel beside the Church of the Nativity," he said, indicating a row of shops next to the courtyard of the church. "This must wait now. A hotel would be a great attraction. All the modern churches are in Jerusalem. We need one. Think how sensational! Visitors could stay close to the exact genuine spot where Jesus Christ was born."

An Arab accosted Walters and me in a dingy café, where we were sharing a bottle of Stella beer, brewed in Egypt. The Arab said he had heard we were journalists. Would we be interested to know that there was much discontent, talk of a strike, in Mayor Canavati's factory? Walters wearily passed over a small sum of money, and we got a small story. It had been suggested that the workers should steal the Christmas bells from the Church of the Nativity at the time of the annual Christmas broadcast, thus calling the attention of the West to the plight of refugee artisans from Palestine.

"What other countries are there?" I asked Walters.

"There's always Lebanon," he replied. "The Switzerland of the Middle East."

We flew to Beirut.

Beirut's a good place to get one's laundry done.

I took a taxi to Aley, a gambling resort in the hills near the capital. I had an appointment to interview ex-Queen Narriman of Egypt, who was living in exile in a villa there.

She looked like a movie starlet who had been eating too many marshmallows. Her face was like a beige silk cushion. She had beautiful, pouting, fat lips—like the mouth of an unhappy Negro angel. She was wearing a skin-tight yellow sweater, a charcoal-gray ballerina skirt, yellow shoes, a gold ring bearing an amethyst the size of a lump of sugar. She sat in a gold-brocaded Empire chair, in front of Flemish tapestry nudes, beneath a glittering chandelier and beside a recent pastel portrait of herself, done before she had changed her hair from ash-blonde to dark red.

She whispered huskily that she had arrived at a momentous decision: she had renounced romantic love for all time. Wasn't twenty-two a bit young to be giving up love? No, she said; she was going to consecrate herself to maternal devotion to her son. Where was he? At the moment he was with his governess, in the Lebanon of Europe.

How did she feel about ex-King Farouk? She said she did not want to throw mud at him, though she was still a little sore about having been forced to leave most of her jewelry and most of her clothes, including an unrivaled collection of lingerie, with his library of erotica in Cairo.

She sighed, and her bust measurement shrank to about 40 inches.

"But I have hopes that President Nasser one day will restore the monarchy—he is very anti-Communist," the ex-Queen said. "And then, of course, my son will be recognized as the King of Egypt."

After some investigation, I was able to report that the beach police at Beirut had revived use of the bastinado to punish men who pinched ladies' bottoms.

I flew to Cyprus.

There was a lot of barbed wire at the airport at Nicosia. An English National Serviceman squeezed my tube of tooth paste, presumably to see whether it contained any dangerous contraband. All it contained was tooth paste, and by the end of the inspection it didn't contain much of that.

"Sorry, sir," the soldier said brightly. "Can't be too careful, though, can we? Not that we suspect you of bringing anything you shouldn't. But EOKA uses all sorts of methods. . . ."

The next day I flew on to Israel.

Menachem Begin, the leader of Herut, Israel's biggest, most militant opposition party, said in Tel Aviv that his colleagues and he were agitating for an all-out attack against Egypt—a preventive war. He believed that his policy would prevail; every night that an Arab "suicide-commando" came across the border with explosives Begin's belief became stronger.

"The best defense is attack," he pointed out.

I flew back to London and met Hugh Gaitskell, the leader of the Labour Party, at a dinner meeting in North Hendon. His primary concern at the moment was Soviet savagery in Hungary. I told him that it looked as though Israel might attack Egypt; but I didn't really convince even myself.

I had been in London almost two days when it was reported that the Israeli Army had just moved into the Sinai Desert. The managing editor sounded surprisingly patient on the telephone. He said that everybody else had been surprised too. At dawn the next day I was in another plane on the way back to Tel Aviv.

Donald Wise, of the London *Daily Express*, said he was glad to see me back, because he needed somebody non-competitive to share the cost of retaining a taxi on call twenty-four hours a day.

"This is a very expensive little war," he said. "You've got to keep your room at the Dan Hotel; you've got to come back to Tel Aviv every night to file. There's no censorship or communications in the field— wherever exactly the field is right now. The Israelis are moving so fast they aren't letting correspondents go all the way forward with them. They're issuing quite good communiqués at headquarters, though, and you can pick up some color in a few hours on the road to the Sinai."

Once again I experienced the mixed feelings, the guilty pleasures, of being a witness without being a partisan at a time of crucial action.

Orange juice, scrambled eggs, hot buttered toast, and black coffee on the balcony of an air-conditioned bedroom overlooking the Mediterranean; a quick swim; then, in sports shirt and Bermuda shorts, with paper and pencil and picnic hamper, off to war in a taxi. . . .

It was an American taxi, two-toned, chrome-laden, with a radio. An enthusiastic Israeli disc jockey was playing everything martial he could lay his hands on. We lolled on soft cushions and the radio blared "Praise the Lord and Pass the Ammunition," as we were driven south, past uniformed women carrying rifles.

We visited a *kibbutz* (collective farm) about half a mile from the Gaza Strip. The Israeli Army was about to take Gaza. Israeli jets flew low over the irrigated green Israeli fields, over the sand dunes and palm groves of Egyptian territory.

"For eight years I have waited to march along the road to Gaza," said an Israeli with fierce blue eyes and a sun-bleached yellow beard. "Today we are going to do so." Wise and I walked with them.

We walked through an Arab village that had been abandoned so hastily that there was burned food on a cooking stove.

There was some machine-gunning, some mortar fire, almost all outgoing. Jets screamed, all "ours." We saw one dead Palestinian Arab soldier.

Another day we drove as far as we were allowed into the Sinai, to within a few miles of the Suez Canal. The roads were littered with destroyed and damaged Soviet equipment.

And we spent each night in the night club of the Dan Hotel. The Tel Aviv blackout made the hotel even more crowded than usual. It was like Miami Beach.

The Israeli Air Force had a victory party in the ballroom. The guests of honor were pilots of the French Air Force. One of them told me that he had flown some strafing missions during the brief campaign in the desert.

The story shifted to the United Nations. In the Israeli sector of Jerusalem, Major General E. L. M. Burns of Canada, who had just been ordered to organize a United Nations Emergency Force to occupy the Suez Canal Zone, advised me to go to Naples to join the first U.N. troops when they assembled there for the journey into Egypt.

I flew to Rome. I rode in a train to Naples. The United Nations spokesman there said that correspondents would have to make their own way into Egypt and could apply in Cairo for accreditation to the U.N.E.F.

The Egyptian consul general, in a decrepit mansion high above the Bay of Naples, suggested a ship from Naples to Bengasi, in Libya, from where one might be able to travel by train and bus to Cairo.

I flew from Naples to Valletta, the capital of Malta. In Malta, I boarded a British European Airways Elizabethan bound for Bengasi. It was like boarding a fantasy by Jean Cocteau. The plane ordinarily carried forty-eight passengers, but that day I was the only one.

The stewardess gave me the customary briefing on how to don a life jacket and offered me barley sugar and ordered me to fasten my seat belt and served drinks, and the captain of the aircraft sent back a position report addressed not to "the passengers" but to me alone.

In Bengasi I chartered a taxi to take me to the Egyptian border. The drive was a delirious one, fast, on broken springs, along a winding switchback road, across a lunar mountainous landscape, in mist and moonlight.

At the border, a few miles west of Salum, by luck I picked up a Cairo taxi that had brought a French refugee out of Egypt and was about to return to the capital. Apart from being arrested as a spy near Alexandria and held for two hours at bayonet-point by a sentry who spoke only Arabic, I reached Cairo uneventfully.

Distance, time, and money by then had lost much of their normal significance. As I recall them now, like memories of hallucinations, the taxis seem to have taken me more or less 1,100 miles in something like 36 hours. The fares amounted to $270. The investment seemed worth making until I reached the Semiramis Hotel on the Nile and saw the vague faces of United Nations officers sitting in the lobby, waiting for an unscheduled special train to an undecided destination.

Fred Sparks, of course, eventually arrived. No international muddle of any importance is complete without him. He looked strangely younger than he had looked in Guatemala.

"The toupée makes a difference," he pointed out. In New York, he had written a column on the advantages of false hair, and America's foremost manufacturer of wigs and toupées had presented him with an extraordinarily realistic Ivy League crew cut, a middle-aged one, grizzled and beginning to grow out and bend flat in front.

Sometimes Sparks wore the toupée; sometimes he left it off. Wearing it, he told strangers in an anxious, confidential whisper that if they ever encountered his older brother in the bar they should not be alarmed: he was perfectly harmless, and he, Sparks-with-hair, would pay any debts that might be incurred by the bald Sparks.

The toupée engendered more drama than was to be detected in the establishment of the United Nations Emergency Force. A chambermaid saw the toupée crouching menacingly on a chair in Spark's bedroom and almost screamed the roof off. Sparks, himself, momentarily panicked when a kite dived at him when he was eating lunch on his balcony. The big bird swooped and grabbed half a chicken off Sparks's plate.

"What a relief," he said afterward. "I thought it was after my hairpiece."

Green passports, not dark blue ones, were in vogue in Cairo that season. In fact, the United States, having done more than any other country, even more than the Soviet Union, to save Nasser's skin, was enjoying a brief period of Egyptian popularity. Correspondents bearing U.S. passports were free to come and go and to work as they pleased. A group of British correspondents, including a couple I had met in Fleet Street, were under house arrest in the Semiramis. During their internment they were still being well fed, at their newspapers' expense, and well treated by their guards—astonishingly well, really, in consideration of what Cairo Radio and the Egyptian press were saying about the Anglo-French bombardment of Port Said; however, the prisoners were bored by confinement. My own British passport having been stored in moth balls only a short time before, I felt that my own position was at once slightly precarious and unjustly privileged. When the British correspondents were escorted by an Egyptian plainclothes officer into the hotel bar each evening, I tried to expiate my feelings of uneasiness by buying them drinks whenever possible, and by loudly discussing with colleagues the events of the day. Anyway, the internment proved to be neither rigorous nor long-lasting; the British correspondents were deported while their editors were still interested in the story of captivity, which was a good deal more interesting, and not much more frustrating, than the articles we other correspondents were writing without restrictions.

The *Statue of Liberty* (an oil tanker) was stuck in the Suez Canal. Sparks and I eventually got permission from the new Egyptian canal authority at Ismailia to go aboard the ship to interview the captain. He was in the middle of reading *War and Peace*.

Captain George Mendes, a Colombian infantry officer, seemed to speak for many of his colleagues, and for several correspondents, when he spoke of Korea as "the good old days."

"There we had authority," he said wistfully. The U.N. felt that it had to show a much more tender regard for Egyptian sovereignty than it had ever shown for the Government of South Korea.

Sparks and I spent an evening sailing a felucca on the Nile. The swarthy captain of the small boat grinned wickedly as his crew, a young boy, handed him his hubbly-bubbly and took over the tiller.

"In the old time," the captain said, settling back in a nest of dirty cushions, "everybody all time go to gay house, gamble, smoke hashish, love gorls. Too much gorls; too much money; verra nice.

"Now Gamal Abdel Nasser say: 'No more gamble, no more hubbly-bubbly, no more gorls.' Gamal Abdel Nasser say: 'Everybody got to work; everybody got to fight for new Egypt.'"

The only people in the new Egypt who continued to indulge in the old vices, the felucca captain concluded (a reliable source?), were the police and officers of the armed forces.

As he lapsed gradually into a blissful stupor, the captain reminisced about the tourists he had entertained aboard his felucca. He said his favorite patrons were rich American women of a certain age. . . .

Even today, if by mischance I walk near a faulty sewer, I see with my inward eye a vision of the Nile; and, on it, a drifting felucca, and, in that, an Egyptian sucking his illicit pipe; and, in the background, a triumphant proclamation of German industrial opportunism, the electric glow of a vast sign in the sky, KRUPP.

There are very few happy memories of the Middle East of that period, and those are overwhelmed by the central fact that justice unfortunately prevailed. Anybody believing in the rule of law, yet not sympathizing with President Nasser, was sure to come away from Egypt feeling schizophrenic in addition to suffering from the famous digestive disorders of the region.

32

The canal was blocked, but life went on. American oil refineries increased their production and their deliveries across the Atlantic. Like most European countries, Britain was able to keep going, with full employment, by imposing only the mildest of restrictions on private motorists. As my wife observed every time she dared to mount the bathroom scales, Britain did not starve.

From my own point of view, 1957 was an idyllic year. Not having taken an official holiday in 1956, I was now entitled to six weeks off; they were like six weeks of vacation from a vacation.

We went skiing in Austria and swimming off Spain. I remember hissing downhill through powder-snow between conifers toward a sunlit Tyrolean village; sipping mulled claret on a terrace as tired feet relaxed inside heavy boots; floating in the Mediterranean, as the sun shone orange through the eyelids; driving past the dull glare of olive groves and eroded rock in the dazzle of midday, into the cool, dim, green tunnel of a sudden avenue of trees; walking between white-washed wineries and peasant cottages and into a dark Catalonian church with a single window of red glass like an inspired shout of revelation.

I knew that I would not mind if I did not attend any more wars and revolutions. My tastes were changing.

We went to Ireland. Technically, I was on duty; there was an election. The campaign did not amount to much; but we awoke in the Shelbourne Hotel and heard gulls crying through white mist over St. Stephen's Green; sunlight and cloud-shadows, amber and purple, flitted alternately over the Wicklow Mountains on a cold and gusty March afternoon; we ate oysters and drank draught stout in small pubs.

I tried to suggest the essence of Irish politics by describing a Sunday morning in Rathangan, a village in the Bog of Allen. Two days before the general election, the populace were far more interested in the outcome of the local church lottery than they were in listening to a speech by Gerard Sweetman, the former Minister of Finance. I don't think the people of Rathangan were peculiar.

It seemed to me that if international enlightenment were the purpose of foreign correspondence, there should be more travelogue in it and relatively less of official communiqués and intelligence from "informed sources" and "diplomatic observers" in capital cities.

Sometimes one had to move with numerous other reporters in a carefully shepherded flock. It was often obviously necessary, and sometimes fascinating, to sit in the press gallery of the house of Commons, especially during the daily preliminary question period ("Is the Minister aware that since the installation of atomic reactors at Windscale there has been a perceptible diminution of migratory flights of wild birds into the surrounding countryside?"), and during major debates, and to attend news briefings in the press offices of the Foreign Office and other ministries, whenever their activities were notably influential.

But for every five days in Westminster and Whitehall, I spent two days elsewhere, often outside London. *The Sun* provided clear justification for this division of time: the London correspondent was supposed to write a Sunday column about odds and ends, not necessarily directly connected with current happenings. The column was called "From a Window in Fleet Street." The title dated from the days when *The Sun* was closely allied, in spirit and operation, with the Manchester *Guardian*. Before moving into the Reuter factory, *The Sun* had always maintained its London bureau in the intellectual atmosphere and physical turmoil of the *Guardian* building at 43 Fleet Street; but the title of the column remained unchanged. The "window" was a magic one: not only could one see around corners with it; its functions were sometimes periscopic and telescopic; it enabled me to scrutinize incidental curiosities from Keflavik to Amman, from Deauville to Tarragona, and from Durham to Widdicombe-in-the-Moor.

Evelyn Waugh told me of his ambition to acquire an elegant Victorian ear-trumpet to replace the utilitarian modern plastic one he was using.

I marched with Vivien Leigh with banners deploring the plan to raze the St. James's Theatre.

Prime Minister Harold Macmillan, showing some guests around Number 10, Downing Street, pointed out structural weaknesses and told me he did not intend to make specific public recommendations to save the building from collapse until he heard the result of the next general election. Now he has won it and a program of extensive restoration is under way.

Yves Klein, a French monochromatic abstractionist, said he was experimenting on the relationships between colors, sounds, and smells. He was working on "a blue smell," and had high hopes of setting it to music.

Anthony Crosland, the socialist economist, fed me steak pie and strawberry mousse in the fellows' dining room at Trinity College, Oxford. Hugh Gaitskell was also present. After lunch the three of us walked to Blackwell's, the bookshop, and Gaitskell asked a salesman for *The Future of Socialism*, an authoritative right-wing Labour Party prognosis written by Crosland, and I heard the salesman mutter to a colleague, "If Gaitskell doesn't know its future, who does?" The question seemed rhetorical at the time.

I had a splendid luncheon with Madame Pandit in her official mansion in Kensington Palace Gardens and she explained the causes of starvation in Indian villages.

I met the Duchess of Marlborough at a reception in celebration of the umpteenth anniversary of one of London's most luxurious and most expensive food and wine stores. She lifted her short speech above platitude, and almost prostrated the directors, by paraphrasing her kinsman, Sir Winston Churchill: "Never before," she said, "have so many paid so much for so little."

Jayne Mansfield told me about having been presented to Queen Elizabeth II at the première of *Les Girls*. "Her eyes were so wonderful with the stones in her crown!" Miss Mansfield exclaimed. "I told her: 'You're so *beautiful!*' and she said: 'Thank you,' and went on to the next person. Eeeeee!" said Miss Mansfield, uttering that special, all-purpose *joie de vivre* squeal that Jane Russell's old director and chapel communicant, Frank Tashlin, had made world famous.

I rode on the merry-go-round at the late Mike Todd's *fête champêtre* in Battersea Pleasure Gardens.

I sailed aboard *Mayflower II* on her first sea trials before her voyage from Plymouth, England, to Plymouth, Massachusetts. Many of the crew were seasick when the ship was towed from the Brixham shipyard along the coast to Plymouth; but Dick Brennan, the second cook, was so proud to be seen in Puritan costume and a beard in the galley that he made me a life member of his London club, the Wig and Pen, which caters principally, as its title is supposed to suggest, to lawyers and journalists. I suppose he wanted me around in future as a witness: I had seen him working.

Secretary Dulles came and went from time to time. Poor old Dulles. I'm sure he always meant well. Certainly he was generous enough, if not always imaginative. I doubt that I'll ever forget Dulles's boyishly enthusiastic presentation of a fishing rod to that ancient tortoise among dictators, President Syngman Rhee, in Seoul. The amusing part of the spectacle was the President's face, the wincing and shuddering of the creased parchment around the mouth, the smile of a man who had just sucked a very sour lemon. He looked as though he was as determined to express appreciation as if his next billion dollars depended on it. In London I never had the pleasure of encountering Dulles in an encouraging mood. His statements on disarmament, which the Big Five (that year's "Big Five") were interminably discussing, were wholly devoid of optimism. But I had to thank him and Harold Stassen and, indeed, the whole United Nations Disarmament Sub-Committee for driving me in desperation to write about disarmament in fantastic terms: they inspired me to write my first piece for *Punch*. Dulles was responsible also for my last visit to Paris as a correspondent for *The Sun*. I went there for Dulles's briefing of American correspondents and to do various other odd jobs while *The Sun*'s military correspondent, the wise and energetic Mark Watson, was attending to the main business at hand, President Eisenhower at the NATO "summit" meeting. The conference, like other NATO meetings, produced an inoffensive communiqué; more important than that, however, the conference afforded the chance to buy a Paris hat for my wife for Christmas. I returned to London with Derek Marks and Richard Kilian, of the *Daily Express*, in the *Golden Arrow*. In train and boat and train the service was consistently excellent: we didn't notice the sea at all.

It is hardly surprising that time seemed to be passing quickly. Suddenly the two-year tour was ending, and the next man in the steadily advancing, heavily breathing queue of would-be London correspondents, Joseph Sterne, was gently, inexorably prying my fingers from the office furniture and bidding for the title of top customer at the Cheshire Cheese. There was no bitterness. Bradford Jacobs had accepted me; I accepted Sterne; Sterne would accept someone else: the process is as inevitable as growing old and dying; a new generation succeeds. Nobody believes that it can really happen to him. But when it does happen he suddenly realizes that he has been half aware all the time of its coming; and so the end of pleasure is also the end of subconscious apprehension.

33

Attending the farewell party was very much like attending the wake after one's own funeral. The party was given by Anthony Crosland in his apartment in South Kensington. "I have invited one or two economists," he had said, "and a young man from Buenos Aires that nobody knows. Their presence will inhibit expressions of sentimentality without cutting down the drinking. I also asked the Finsbury Park ceramist, but she said that when you helped her to move you tried to pack her in a suitcase, so she won't come."

Eventually, about sixteen or twenty people were gathered together, including the Gaitskells, Lady Jane Heaton, who is a pilot and singer of Russian folk songs, and Robert Kee, an amiable Jekyll-Hyde figure, a novelist who frequently metamorphoses into a BBC television commentator. Ella Fitzgerald, hot, sweet, robust, sang tirelessly until somebody fell into the phonograph. By four o'clock, after the Gaitskells had gone, Kee goaded everybody else on: "That's right; that's it; go ahead and blub!" To blub is English schoolboy slang meaning to cry, and therefore blubbing, as distinguished from ordinary crying, is a form of emotional release suitable for people who believe they have stiff upper lips. By the time of confused dispersal some of the faces, we were gratified to notice, were moistening a bit, while the young man from Buenos Aires brokenheartedly exchanged addresses with the prettier guests.

Susan and I fully perceived the magnitude of our grief later that morning when the airplane roared and rattled like a lawnmower along the wet concrete of London Airport. Across the English Channel we sweated in the blue and golden dazzle of the sky above and the white glare of clouds below. There was a luncheon of cellophane and rubber and warm gin. I thought the tears would never stop. Our small daughters, Sheila and Ellen Craig, were quite patient.

A long pink car carried us in our quiet, miserable convulsions along the inland road to Cannes. At Gourdon, a perched village noted in the Michelin guide with those small radiant lines like surprised eyelashes that signify panoramic splendor, the driver made us buy scent. It was not immediately thrilling to learn that in Bond Street it would have cost more. Our faces having been buried again in cushions, again our shoulders heaved.

From the balcony of our bedroom in a white palace glittering with chandeliers and mirrors, we surveyed the Croisette, the beach, and the Mediterranean Sea. Next day we were to sail for Naples, Gibraltar, and New York.

The telephone rang. A small metallic voice said it was Croydon aerodrome calling. It had been instructed to request us to be in our hotel at 11:30 that night. Mr. Crosland and Lady Jane had chartered a plane, we were told, and they were already on the way down from London and would be disappointed, they had said, if we could not join them for supper.

Tony arrived looking very tired in a crumpled brown tweed suit. Jane was still wearing a plain black cocktail dress.

"I'll have to pretend I'm in mourning," she said, wrinkling her big, pale, handsome face in the manner of laughter. It was impossible to detect desperation through her opaque black sunglasses, but there was a hint of urgency when she added, "D'you think we could have some Pernod quite soon?"

In a small all-night restaurant, we ate soup full of heads and tentacles and drank a certain amount of various things and composed an obituary account of the party. It was Tony's opinion that no party was satisfactorily completed, not even a farewell party, without a thorough analytical gossip at the end.

Shortly after noon we reassembled. There was a dreadful pallor about Tony's shave and Jane's mourning cocktail dress now looked authentically funereal. My wife and I didn't closely examine each other, so delicately sensitive seemed the hair triggers of our dyspepsia. But as we walked, as though on tightropes, between the sunlit palms and flowers along the Croisette, and looked at the white yachts on the blue water, we felt gradually suffused with the warm and gentle and light sentimentality that the Mediterranean brings to Northern hearts, and even to Northern minds. There was a P. G. Wodehousean blitheness, an innocent bliss, about the place that day. The casino looked like a shrine.

"It really is jolly nice, isn't it?" Jane said, removing her sunglasses. It really was.

"How long do you think you'll be able to stay down?" I asked Tony.

"Not very long, I'm afraid. I've got an appointment in London at 7:30, and Jane's got a dinner to go to."

Neither of them being actually rich, the sacrificial enormity of their gesture impressed us so deeply that our selfish sorrow lessened further.

We had a strangely casual lunch, under a big blue umbrella, on a pale-peach tessellated terrace. When the two taxis separated, theirs heading for Nice Airport, ours for the Gare Maritime, they and we were waving through the back windows quite cheerfully.

34

In the train from New York to Baltimore I recalled the first time
I had undertaken that journey, a little more than ten years before, on
my way to ask Dorsey for a job. What had been achieved since then?

I had wanted to travel as a reporter; and I had traveled about
85,000 miles, not counting the mileage between *The Sun* news room
and the Calvert Bar & Grill. I had wanted to write as a reporter; and
I had written about two million words, some of which I was able
to reread without regret after publication. Every reporter must acknowledge that there have been times when he has seen in print
something of his own and modesty has failed to prevent him from
saying to himself, "Man, that really sings!" I admit there have been
such times. Just a few of them, now and then, have helped to make
up for the intervening dull gray periods.

But were the stamps in the passports and the clippings (already
yellowing) in the scrapbooks enough? Surely it was time to establish
something substantial. Some of my contemporaries already owned
split-level ranch houses and were active in the parent-teachers asso-

ciation. Tiny fists hammered my head: it was being called to my attention that the train was crossing a bridge. Well, I had acquired a wife and two children. Perhaps we could take out Blue Cross and Blue Shield and settle down.

One of the characteristics of journalism, however, as I realized then, is that the more good assignments you get, the more you feel you need. After what Dorsey, after rye Old Fashioneds in the Maryland Club two years earlier, had called "the big time," meaning the London Bureau, the readjustment to local reporting in Baltimore was going to be more difficult than ever before. Once you get used to main-lining, smoking reefers loses much of its charm, and chewing bubble gum seems to be out of the question. How was he going to keep us down on the farm, after we'd seen Paree? That was Dorsey's problem, as I saw it. But I was soon to discover that Dorsey saw it quite differently, if, indeed, he acknowledged that there was a problem. Perhaps he did not care whether we stayed down on the farm or not. There was an ample supply of applications from enthusiastic aspirant reporters who could be had at apprentice salaries.

The old gang on the fifth floor of the air-conditioned red-brick factory at Calvert & Centre Streets had not significantly changed. Some of the people were different, of course—as usual, some had died and some had gone to work for television, and there were some new young men in Ivy League-type dark suits; but essentially it was the same old gang, valorously whispering about going out on strike any week if conditions didn't get better soon.

There was old Hal Gardner, the drama critic. He reviewed plays, very intelligently, whenever he could find one in town, but that was not often. Most of the time he reviewed movies. He privately gave the impression that in his nostrils most movies stank; but at least he had an office of his own and, more important, he had autonomy. There was old James Bready, a prematurely round-shouldered writer of minor editorials, who seemed to be content gradually filling his cubicle with a magpie collection of out-of-date periodicals and obscure anecdotes about his acquaintances. There was old John Goodspeed, writing a humorous daily column as merrily as a lifer sewing mailbags. There was old Bob Breen, who had a genius for discovering spinsters who collected antique embroidered earmuffs, and always in the remoter reaches of the State: reporters were allowed ten cents a mile to operate their automobiles on duty. There was old Weldon Wallace, who stood foursquare against illiteracy and cancer and did not care who knew it. There was old Charlie Whiteford. . . . But enough; suffice it to say that some of my colleagues seemed to be friends, some not, but almost all of them seemed to have come to terms with their jobs and they were continuing to do them just as they had been doing them before. As I returned after my longest absence I experienced an overwhelming sense of *déjà vu* and also *déjà* fed to the teeth. Surely one could not repeatedly go back to the beginning again as though a career were only a game of snakes and ladders, could one? Apparently, one could. I was required to submit myself once more to the kindergarten discipline of the city desk.

Clarence Caulfield, an assistant city editor whom I dearly loved, looked up from a batch of last year's clippings that had just come to light again in the come-up file. After something has occurred in Baltimore on the same date two years in a row *The Sun* refers to it as a "traditional annual event" and a reporter and a photographer are assigned to record its repeated occurrences for evermore. This practice is like perpetual care in a prosperous cemetery.

"Hi, Pat," Caulfield said, the dear leprechaun, his eyes twinkling over his spectacles. A few more silver threads among the carrot, I noticed, but otherwise he looked blessedly unchanged. He was wearing the cottage-industry green woolen tie that I had sent him from Dublin. It was good to see him. He stood up and reached out a hand. "I was just telling Pat Furgurson here about an excellent meal I had in Cumberland one time when I was traveling through that way, when I was in the feed business," he said. He was often nostalgic for those spacious, leisurely days, especially when he was face to face with a deadline. Ah, yes, that brought tears to the eyes; he always told that one well; for a moment I was pleased to be there. "Well," Caulfield said, "I'm glad to see you're back in good time to cover the Flower Mart."

Seventeen glasses of ouzo later, under the benign, lugubrious surveillance of James Margaritis, then the proprietor of the Calvert, and in the company of the aforementioned Furgurson, a new reporter who,

I soon discovered, was loaded with talent, I was still unable to wash from my consciousness the facts that the forty-sixth annual Flower Mart was soon to be held in Mount Vernon Place and that I would be writing about it.

"That Flower Mart bit, that's the most," Furgurson said, weakly slapping his thigh. "Yeah, that's a real swingin' assignment, man! Crazy!" He cackled like to bust, so I dried my eyes and tried to see things in their true proportions, that is, *The Sun* very big and me very small.

Actually, in all fairness, I must record that my first real assignment on resuming my cotton-picking labors in the local fields was to interview a Customs appraiser on his ruling that a dozen abstractions painted by Congo, a two-and-a-half-year-old chimpanzee, could not be exempted from duty as works of art. This chimpanzee used to do his painting in the London Zoo, see? so my experience was not being wasted, after all.

I wrote about the Preakness Stakes, the Maryland Hunt Cup, and the preparations that John D. Schapiro, the president of Laurel Race Course, and Joe Cascarella, the vice president, were making to add Russian horses to the Washington (D.C.) International Stakes, thus turning that year's race into a skirmish of the cold war. I wrote about a fashion show at the Maryland Reformatory for Women, about painting and poetry and how to prepare snails for the table, about an acrobat's attempt to set a new pole-sitting record and about Governor McKeldin's opposition to capital punishment.

At about this point, by midsummer, 1958, I was having some quite harrowing discussions with my shaving mirror. "*Quo vadis?*" I would ask myself. "*Quo* indeed?" the answer would come back. I began looking through back numbers of the *Reader's Digest* for reassuring articles about cases of the precocious onset of the male menopause. I couldn't find any. Was this curtains?

Two men above all helped me from total despondency. One of them was A. D. Emmart, an editor of the *Evening Sun*, who had been encouraging me for years, even when my output had been nugatory, and who continued to do so now at this time of self-doubt. I am grateful to him. The other was Ned Burks, who had been the paper's Bonn correspondent while I had been in London, and who was in exactly the same situation as I was. I felt sure that he had done well in Germany, and so I was able occasionally to persuade myself that our present status was not so much a deliberate punishment as a sign of casual neglect; evidently it could have been a result of *The Sun*'s having more correspondents than bureaus and of the reluctance of the paper's business administration to acknowledge, except, of course, to advertisers, that the recession was over and that the news department could well afford to send reporters to parts of the world where there weren't any.

Burks and I surveyed the situation. *The Sun* had bureaus in London, Moscow, Bonn, Rome, and Washington. We considered them one by one, and their incumbents, and one by one the bureaus seemed immediately, absolutely, hopelessly inaccessible as far as we were concerned. The situation was bad. What could we hope for in the future? When would Dorsey send a man to the Far East? But what did it matter? When he did, he would send Philip Potter, and quite rightly. How about establishing an office in Panama City or Rio from which to cover Latin America? Apart from the New York *Times* and, on Jules Dubois' better days, the Chicago *Tribune*, North American newspapers seemed to be making no serious attempt to cover Latin America. But Dorsey usually remained curiously indifferent to that region, except occasionally at times of revolutionary chaos, and then it was often too late.

"You know what, Catling?" Burks said, having completed the analysis.

"What?"

"We are screwed."

He seemed to have something there, which Nathan Miller, another colleague, for one, eagerly confirmed.

"Don't forget, when you're ready to quit," Miller reminded me, "I was the first to ask for your desk."

Burks bought miniature bottles of bourbon and we got *The Sun* guard to unlock the door to the roof and we went up and looked for the latest Sputnik. One night we actually saw it. (It was not until many months later that I learned of his well deserved escape to the New York *Times*.)

Felix Goldsborough, my step-father, invited my family to spend our summer holiday with him and my mother on the Eastern Shore. We swam from his boat and water-skied and played croquet and ate terrapin and crabs and I did some writing, and in the evenings we sat around in a beatific digestive coma in the flickering glow of television Westerns.

One morning, after swimming had cooled my head, everything suddenly became very clear.

"There are other newspapers!" I shouted.

I sat right down with pen in hand and addressed myself to Gerard Fay, the London editor of the Manchester *Guardian*, that most humane of daily magazines, which looks just like a newspaper.

Dorsey, inscrutable to the last, wrote an extraordinarily kind letter to whom it might concern, in which he gave me credit for all those professional qualities that I had recently assumed he must have found lacking in me.

Gerard Fay said I should come on over.

James M. Cannon III would have been proud of me. We sailed first class. And we're living happily ever after, I think. Anyway, it's better than working.

World's End,
Chelsea, 1960